CRIMINAL JUSTICE PLANNING

CRIMINAL JUSTICE PLANNING

PLANNING

An Introduction

DON C. GIBBONS

JOSEPH L. THIMM

FLORENCE YOSPE

GERALD F. BLAKE, JR.

School of Urban Affairs, Portland State University

Prentice-Hall, Inc., Englewood Cliffs, New Jersey 07632

Library of Congress Cataloging in Publication Data
Main entry under title:

Criminal justice planning.

    Includes bibliographical references and index.
    1. Criminal justice, Administration of—Planning—United States.
I. Gibbons, Don C.
HV8138.C69   364′.973   76-51464
ISBN 0-13-193037-0

Printed in the United States of America

10 9 8 7 6 5 4 3 2 1

Prentice-Hall International, Inc., *London*
Prentice-Hall of Australia Pty. Limited, *Sydney*
Prentice-Hall of Canada, Ltd., *Toronto*
Prentice-Hall of India Private Limited, *New Delhi*
Prentice-Hall of Japan, Inc., *Tokyo*
Prentice-Hall of Southeast Asia Pte. Ltd., *Singapore*
Whitehall Books Limited, *Wellington, New Zealand*

Contents

Preface

Social planning has been a feature of modern societies for many decades, with urban and regional planning, economic planning, and demographic planning constituting some of its most well known forms. Planning within the criminal justice system, however, is of recent origin and probably qualifies as the newest brand of social planning.

This book traces some of the factors that have given rise to criminal justice planning. For one, current levels of lawbreaking appear to be so high that the law enforcement, judicial, and correctional system is likely to collapse within the next decade or so from the weight of numbers unless greater coordination of the crime control efforts of various parts of the system is achieved and unless comprehensive planning for innovative responses to the crime problem is developed. Partly to address this problem, the United States Congress, through the Omnibus Crime Control and Safe Streets Act of 1968 and the creation of the Law Enforcement Assistance Administration, has placed great emphasis upon the establishment of state planning agencies. To be eligible for federal funds for crime fighting, states must engage in planning efforts.

Given the newness of criminal justice planning, it is no wonder that it is not yet much more than an immature field of planning practice. The criminal justice planning literature currently in existence consists of a number of hortatory essays urging us to begin to engage in planning, along with a few broad conceptual statements in which terminology from other fields of planning has been applied to the criminal justice field. Additionally, a variety of specific methodological techniques that might be employed by justice planners have been discussed, such as Offender-Based Transaction Statistics. Finally, at least two monographs on planning have made their appearance, but they have a number of limitations that we shall take up in this book.

This book represents a beginning effort at an introductory but comprehensive discussion of justice system planning. The reader will encounter a generous sampling of the existing literature on planning in these pages, along with our own efforts to identify some of the major directions that criminal justice system planning ought to pursue.

We devote a good deal of space in this book to commentary on incremental planning. We advocate the development of increasingly more useful plans through a process of successive approximations in which plans are developed, tried out, and modified in the light of new experience. In somewhat the same way, we view this brief book as an initial venture into development of planning technology which will ultimately be replaced by more comprehensive and sophisticated works. Indeed, we will regard our efforts as successful if they stimulate others to develop planning perspectives and methodology that will make this volume obsolete within a few years.

This book is a product of the curriculum development activities carried on during 1975–76 within the National Criminal Justice Educational Development Project at Portland State University. That project centered on development of a doctoral program in criminal justice within the School of Urban Affairs and was funded by the Law Enforcement Assistance Administration. However, the views expressed here are our own and do not necessarily represent the official position or policies of the U.S. Department of Justice.

About the authors: Don C. Gibbons is Professor of Sociology and Urban Studies; Joseph L. Thimm is Lecturer in Urban Studies and Manager, Office of Planning and Evaluation, in the State of Oregon Children's Services Division; Florence Yospe is a Research Associate in the Criminal Justice Educational Development Project; and Gerald F. Blake is Assistant Professor of Sociology and Urban Studies. We hope that this blend of backgrounds and experiences is reflected in this book, for our intent has been to merge the world of theory with the world of practice in our discussions of planning.

We received a good deal of encouragement and assistance from a number of persons while preparing this manuscript. Michael Wiatrowski, James White, Bradley Q. Post, Richard Whipple, David Johnson, and Kathryn Farr, doctoral candidates in the criminal justice program, all contributed to the book. Professor Vincent O'Leary, Dr. Sumner Sharpe, Dr. William Harris, and Mr. John Galvin read earlier versions of the material and offered helpful suggestions for its improvement. We are most heavily indebted to Dr. Peter G. Garabedian for a number of detailed, substantive criticisms which we have attempted to address in the final version of the manuscript. Finally, Ms. Kathy Grove typed the entire manuscript. Her skillful and diligent efforts made this undertaking much less difficult than it might have otherwise been.

Portland, Oregon   Don C. Gibbons

Joseph L. Thimm

Florence Yospe

Gerald F. Blake, Jr.

CRIMINAL JUSTICE PLANNING

1

The Planning Challenge

INTRODUCTION

During the past few years, a number of observers of the contemporary criminal justice scene have issued diagnoses of the problems of the criminal and juvenile justice machinery, holding that this apparatus is dangerously close to collapse.[1] These same commentators have argued that if present crime trends continue, and if the justice operation does not undergo major alterations, total breakdown of that system is inevitable. For example, Herbert Sigurdson, Robert Carter, and A. W. McEachern have produced estimates of crime in the Los

---

[1] For example, see Ronald I. Weiner, "The Criminal Justice System at the Breaking Point," *Social Work*, 20 (November 1975), 436–41.

Angeles area for the year 2000 and have contended that unless major changes occur in the law enforcement, judicial, and correctional structures, "the criminal justice system will, in fact, collapse from sheer input and uncoordinated processing of offenders." [2] In all of these assessments of the prospects for the criminal justice machinery, the authors end up arguing that comprehensive criminal justice planning is urgently required if we are to avert disaster.

The National Council on Crime and Delinquency has spoken at length on the need for comprehensive criminal justice planning.[3] A policy statement by the board of directors of that organization, issued in 1974, begins with the following proposition:

> Comprehensive criminal justice planning at the local, state, and national level is essential for the reduction and control of delinquency and crime. Focusing on the criminal justice system as a whole, the planning process must be expertly carried out; must involve citizens, social and behavioral scientists, and ex-offenders in addition to the officials and technicians who operate the system; must coordinate allocations of federal, state, and local tax funds; and must insure that the cost-effectiveness of all criminal justice programs will be continually and objectively evaluated.[4]

This policy statement goes on to advocate the establishment of criminal justice planning as a permanent operation within state government, inclusion of juvenile justice system planning within that operation, development of regional planning activities, and careful selection of qualified planning staff. Also, the policy statement argues for the establishment of a National Planning Commission as a permanent body that would be charged with developing strategies for coordinating federal grant programs relating to crime and delinquency. This national commission would also provide high-level leadership to the search for new ideas and approaches to lawbreaking.

---

[2] Herbert R. Sigurdson, Robert M. Carter, and A. W. McEachern, "Methodological Impediments to Comprehensive Criminal Justice Planning," *Criminology, 9* (August–November 1971), 248–67.

[3] "Comprehensive Criminal Justice Planning: A Policy Statement," *Crime and Delinquency, 20* (January 1974), 10–14. The need for justice system planning has also been emphasized by the National Advisory Commission on Criminal Justice Standards and Goals in *A National Strategy to Reduce Crime* (Washington, D.C., 1973).

[4] Ibid., p. 10.

Until relatively recently, long-range and comprehensive planning has been little evident in any component part of the criminal justice field. Indeed, even the short-range planning that occurred was generally ad hoc, often in response to some immediate crisis facing the organization or agency. This point has been underscored by one observer of the criminal justice process:

> The main problem seems to be that individual criminal justice agencies tend to be reactive rather than future-oriented in their decision making and operations. Systematic and comprehensive long-range planning is seldom done because these agencies are constantly being subjected to short-term political pressures; their funding is based on a one-year cycle; and the problems of the moment are often real enough and quite compelling.[5]

However, the passage of the Omnibus Crime Control and Safe Streets Act of 1968 and the creation of the Law Enforcement Assistance Administration (LEAA) have given considerable impetus to the development of systematic planning processes and to the emergence of criminal justice planning as a profession. The individual states are required by the crime control act to have statewide planning agencies which are intended as devices for bringing about the wisest use of federal funds. Among other tasks, the state planning agency is required to prepare a comprehensive statewide plan for the use of LEAA block grant funds. Additionally, justice planners are employed in the planning districts within each state. Currently about two thousand persons are involved in these positions as criminal justice planners.

CRIMINAL JUSTICE PLANNING AS A PROFESSION

The policy statement of the National Council on Crime and Delinquency argued that criminal justice planning should be of the highest possible quality:

---

[5] Burt Nanus, "A General Model for Criminal Justice Planning," *Journal of Criminal Justice*, 2 (Winter 1974), 346.

> Planning staff should be carefully selected to obtain the professional skills needed for designing criminal justice programs and for evaluating and monitoring services and expenditures. LEAA should finance in-service training for criminal justice planning personnel, and universities should be encouraged to develop curricula for criminal justice planning.[6]

It seems doubtful that anyone could fault this recommendation for skilled planning. But, given the rapid emergence of justice planner occupational roles, we might ask about the professional status of criminal justice planning.

What is a "profession"? Social scientists tend to agree on a common definition of the core ingredients or elements of professions. Moreover, most laymen hold implicit notions of professionalism that parallel the more formalized views of sociologists and other social scientists. For example, Ernest Greenwood has argued that professions are characterized by (a) a body of systematic theory shared by the members, (b) authority recognized by the clientele of the professional group, (c) a code of ethics governing relations of professional persons with clients and fellow professionals, and (d) a professional culture sustained by formal professional associations.[7] These elements are found in their most highly developed form in such professions as law, medicine, engineering, and dentistry, while they are almost totally absent from such occupations as those involving truck drivers or apartment house maintenance men. Most laymen would be quick to acknowledge that their physician is a professional but would be loath to accord professional status to their janitor, regardless of whether he labeled himself a janitor or a "maintenance engineer." In short, persons do not become bona fide professionals simply by claiming professional status.[8]

---

[6] "Comprehensive Criminal Justice Planning," p. 11.

[7] Ernest Greenwood, "Attributes of a Profession," Social Work, 2 (July 1957), 44–55. Also see Howard M. Vollmer and Donald L. Mills, eds., Professionalism (Englewood Cliffs, N.J.: Prentice-Hall, 1966).

[8] In recent years, many persons have characterized law enforcement as a profession. However, one would be hard pressed to argue the case that police work is a profession within the definition offered by Greenwood. Instead, it bears more similarity to a craft, that is, a skilled trade or occupation.

Jerome Skolnick has characterized police work as a craft and has provided a detailed analysis of the craft aspects of police work in a large West Coast city. See Skolnick, Justice without Trial (New York: John Wiley, 1966). James Q. Wilson

Now, what of criminal justice planning as a profession? We shall take up criminal justice planning activities in detail in Chapter 2, where we will see that the justice planning that has been carried on in recent years has not been markedly impressive in terms of comprehensiveness or impact upon justice system operations. In this opening chapter, however, it is sufficient to note the fundamental fact that justice planning is still in its infancy, so that a comprehensive body of theory, practice knowledge, and skills which can be pointed to as the corpus of a criminal justice planning profession does not yet exist. One cannot yet identify a collection of individuals who can be said to be skilled, professional justice planners. Instead, state and district planning positions are currently staffed by a heterogeneous collection of persons with disparate backgrounds and training who often have only a relatively rudimentary grounding in planning.

The field of criminal justice planning is currently quite similar to the urban planning of several decades ago. An earlier generation of city planners was drawn heavily from the ranks of architects, and also included a number of persons with a mixture of educational backgrounds in social science disciplines. City planners often exhibited slavish allegiance to notions of urban design revolving around neigh-

---

shares this view of the nature of police work. See Wilson, *Varieties of Police Behavior* (Cambridge: Harvard University Press, 1968). In one place (p. 30), he observes that "members of professions tend to govern themselves through collegial bodies, to restrict the authority of their nominal superiors, to take seriously their reputation among fellow professionals, and to encourage some of their kind to devote themselves to adding systematically to the knowledge of the profession through writing and research. The police are not in any of these senses professionals. They acquire most of their knowledge and skill on the job, not in separate academies; they are emphatically subject to the authority of their superiors; they have no serious professional society, only a union-like bargaining agent; and they do not produce, in systematic written form, new knowledge about their craft."

In an insightful discussion of police "professionalization," Skolnick points out that police officials usually have in mind a narrow conception of professionalism emphasizing managerial efficiency and bureaucratization of police work. He argues that it is not possible, in fact, for the police to operate solely on the basis of bureaucratic rules, and even more important, that this narrow view of professionalism blinds police administrators to their responsibility to encourage police compliance to the rule of law. See Skolnick, *Justice without Trial*, pp. 235–45.

For a summary of other studies of policing, see Don C. Gibbons, *Society, Crime and Criminal Careers*, 3rd ed. (Englewood Cliffs, N.J.: Prentice-Hall, 1977), pp. 49–77. Vollmer and Mills, in *Professionalism*, acknowledge that professionalism is a matter of degree, so that some organizations and occupations are more professional than others. On this point, Wilson has identified a number of types of police agencies, some of which operate more legalistically and bureaucratically than others. See Wilson, *Varieties of Police Behavior*.

borhood concepts, in which the city was divided into communities centered on a core comprised of an elementary or a secondary school. Much of this early city planning was uninformed by detailed knowledge of urban land economics, ecological patterns and processes, or the findings of urban sociology and geography. In short, city planning has only recently grown from a relatively crude art form into a profession based upon a solid underpinning of valid knowledge about urban phenomena.[9]

There is a dearth of writing available on justice planning, either in book form or in the various criminological and criminal justice journals, which is a clear sign that justice planning is an embryonic profession in search of a body of technical knowledge and special skills upon which professional practice principles might be constructed. At the same time, the question of the knowledge base of a criminal justice planning profession has received increased attention in recent years. Essays and monographs on criminal justice planning have appeared, in which some of the major problems of planning and some components of planning knowledge have been identified. Planning curricula of the kind called for by the National Council on Crime and Delinquency have been developed; indeed, this book grew out of one such curriculum development endeavor. In short, although criminal justice planning is in its infancy, definite signs of growth toward maturity can be discerned. This book is intended as a contribution to the emerging literature upon which a criminal justice planning profession can be nurtured.

PROLOGUE

This book is concerned with stocktaking regarding the current state of the art in criminal justice planning. In the chapters that follow, a generous sampling of the commentary that has been produced to date on the problems and major ingredients of planning is examined, along with our own explication of the dimensions of planning knowledge that need further development. More specifically, Chapter 2 takes up the current state of criminal justice planning,

---

[9] For a detailed discussion of the development of American city planning, see Mel Scott, *American City Planning Since 1890* (Berkeley: University of California Press, 1969).

tracing the developments that have grown out of federal crime-fighting legislation in the 1960s. This chapter also includes a detailed discussion of criminal justice planning efforts in several states.

Chapter 3 focuses on organizational problems that have plagued efforts at justice planning in the past and which promise to continue to complicate the planner's task in the future. The component agencies of the criminal justice "system" often operate with different mandates or tasks which they endeavor to perform. For example, the police view their job as centered on crime reduction and often regard the courts or correctional agencies as working at cross-purposes to them. Moreover, the police, courts, and correctional agencies do, in fact, pursue somewhat discordant goals. In addition, the various functionaries within the justice system often exhibit divergent value perspectives and differing beliefs about crime and criminals, such that it is often difficult to maintain the contention that the criminal justice apparatus in its entirety does truly constitute a system.

Chapter 4 reviews a large share of the literature that has emerged regarding criminal justice planning, in which various conceptual frameworks centering on systems analysis have been put forth. Chapters 5 and 6 continue this line of commentary, but with emphasis upon our own conceptual framework for criminal justice planning. Chapter 5 presents a discussion of theories and evidence on crime causation, along with findings growing out of evaluative studies of correctional programs. Among other things, Chapter 6 explores the utility of a number of planning concepts adopted from other areas of social planning.

Chapter 7 continues the discussion of planning viewpoints and practices, but with emphasis upon planning resources and methodology. This chapter also includes commentary on data sources; system rates, modeling, and simulation techniques; program evaluation methodology; and a number of other tools for the justice system planner. The final chapter presents a relatively brief analysis of some of the organizational dimensions of planning as a social process, indicating some of the directions to be pursued as we gear up for criminal justice planning on an increased scale.

Our analysis in this book avoids technical jargon, esoteric statistical techniques, and the like. This volume is intended to serve as a sourcebook and reference text for criminal justice planners and neophyte planners, most of whom need to be introduced to the basic literature on planning before launching into more complex and arcane topics.

2

The Current State of Criminal Justice Planning

INTRODUCTION

Chapter 1 commented upon the underdeveloped state of criminal justice planning as a profession and noted that this type of planning is an occupational specialization of recent origin. Chapter 1 also observed that justice planning is a burgeoning specialization that has been given considerable impetus by federal crime-fighting legislation. In this chapter, we examine the origins of crime control legislation and the planning mandate contained in that legislation; assess the performance of the Law Enforcement Assistance Administration, state planning agencies, and local planning units in justice planning that has occurred to date; and report some specific observations on the planning experiences in selected states, including a detailed account of planning operations in the state of Oregon. This chapter comprises a review of criminal justice planning practice as it has evolved over the past dozen years in the United States and provides a background against which to place the explication of conceptual, theoretical, and methodological issues in justice planning to be considered in subsequent chapters.

FEDERAL CRIME-FIGHTING LEGISLATION

The War on Crime

Federal legislative action inaugurating a "war on crime" was rooted in the larger social, economic, and political events of the early sixties. While the President's Commission on Law Enforcement and Administration of Justice is usually identified as the precursor of the Omnibus Crime Control and Safe Streets Act of 1968, the climate of the country in the years preceding the enactment of that legislation also warrants attention.

Federal government efforts to deal with the national crime problem began in 1965 when President Johnson created the Commission on Law Enforcement and Administration of Justice. The commission and its staff conducted the most comprehensive and searching study of crime in American society ever undertaken by the federal government. The summary report of the commission contains over two hundred recommendations for control and prevention of crime.[1] The president's commission report warned against facile proposals for the cure of crime which aim to come down hard on various groups in society, and it rejected those palliatives and proposed solutions that would escalate the hostility between society and its criminals. The report pointed to major renovations in the American social structure rather than at some minor tinkering. The summary passages from the report called for a broad and comprehensive attack on the "root causes" of crime, involving such steps as reduction of unemployment, improvements in the educational system, and amelioration of urban squalor and blight. As Richard Harris has indicated:

---

[1] The President's Commission on Law Enforcement and Administration of Justice, *The Challenge of Crime in a Free Society* (Washington, D.C.: Government Printing Office, 1967).

Like other crime studies, this one showed "that most crimes, wherever they are committed, are committed by boys and young men, and that most crimes, by whomever they are committed, are committed in cities." The facts were not particularly surprising, but to many readers the Commission's conclusions were. While it recommended immediate steps to upgrade the quality of the police and their methods, to revise outdated court systems, and to improve correctional techniques, it repeatedly stated that a lasting solution would require widespread recognition of basic matters that had long been overlooked or ignored and the development of a comprehensive program that would take as much money and understanding as the nation could muster.[2]

The Omnibus Crime Control Act

The commission recommendations, however, did not culminate in a massive and wide-ranging initiative against crime and its basic causes. Instead, President Johnson's proposal for crime legislation eventually led to the passage of the Omnibus Crime Control and Safe Streets Act of 1968, along with subsequent amendments. This act was not designed to bring about major reforms in the criminal justice system. Rather, it was a response to current fears of crime, agitation regarding urban riots in ghetto areas, and hostility toward the Supreme Court for allegedly tying the hands of the police through such decisions as *Mallory* and *Miranda*.[3] The crime control bill modified the *Miranda* ruling by allowing all "voluntary" confessions to be accepted as evidence in federal courts. It also provided for admission of all police lineup identifications in federal cases, regardless of whether the accused person was represented by an attorney at the lineup. The measure also allowed for delay between arrest and charge, reversing *Mallory*.

In his introduction to the Harris book, former Attorney General Nicholas Katzenbach asserts that civil rights activities, ghetto riots, radical student demonstrations, anti-Vietnam acts of protest, and Supreme Court decisions all played a role in establishing the connection, in the public's mind, between the rise in street crime and other forms of civil disorder. Furthermore, these perceptions made it

---

[2] Richard Harris, *The Fear of Crime* (New York: Praeger, 1968), pp. 15–16.

[3] Ibid.

impossible for the crime problem to be discussed and acted upon rationally by the Congress, as the president's commission had attempted to do. Thus the translation of recommendations from the commission into the enactment of the Omnibus Crime Control and Safe Streets Act of 1968 represented a failure both on the part of Congress and on the part of the intellectual leaders to communicate with a large segment of the American public.

The Law Enforcement Assistance Administration

Federal funding of crime-fighting activities was provided for in the crime control bill, specifically through the creation of the Law Enforcement Assistance Administration (the organizational structure of LEAA is shown in Figure 1). That agency began with a budget of $63 million in 1969, which grew to $268 million in 1970 and $529 million in 1971, and the fifteen-month budget for fiscal 1976 was $1 billion (the LEAA budget history is shown in Figure 2, and the division of funds in spending categories is shown in Figure 3). LEAA spending was projected at a somewhat reduced figure for 1977. Although at first glance it might appear that substantial federal funding has been devoted to crime-reduction measures, the 1976 LEAA expenditures of approximately $770 million represent only a small portion of the total federal budget in excess of $300 billion.

The lion's share of the LEAA budget is reallocated to the individual states through the Part C "block grant" program, in which they determine how the moneys are to be spent. Only a small part of the LEAA budget is devoted to discretionary funds through which the federal agency is able to sponsor special projects and innovative crime-reduction efforts. Part E funds shown in Figure 3 represent moneys earmarked for correctional programs, while the other categories involve funds that are utilized by LEAA for other special purposes.

LEAA: Some Critical Views

Newspaper columnist Jack Anderson has been a vociferous critic of LEAA in recent years, and many other persons have also found fault with this program. The most extreme criticism comes from radical criminologists such as Richard Quinney, who holds that the agency is a tool of the ruling class through which repression of

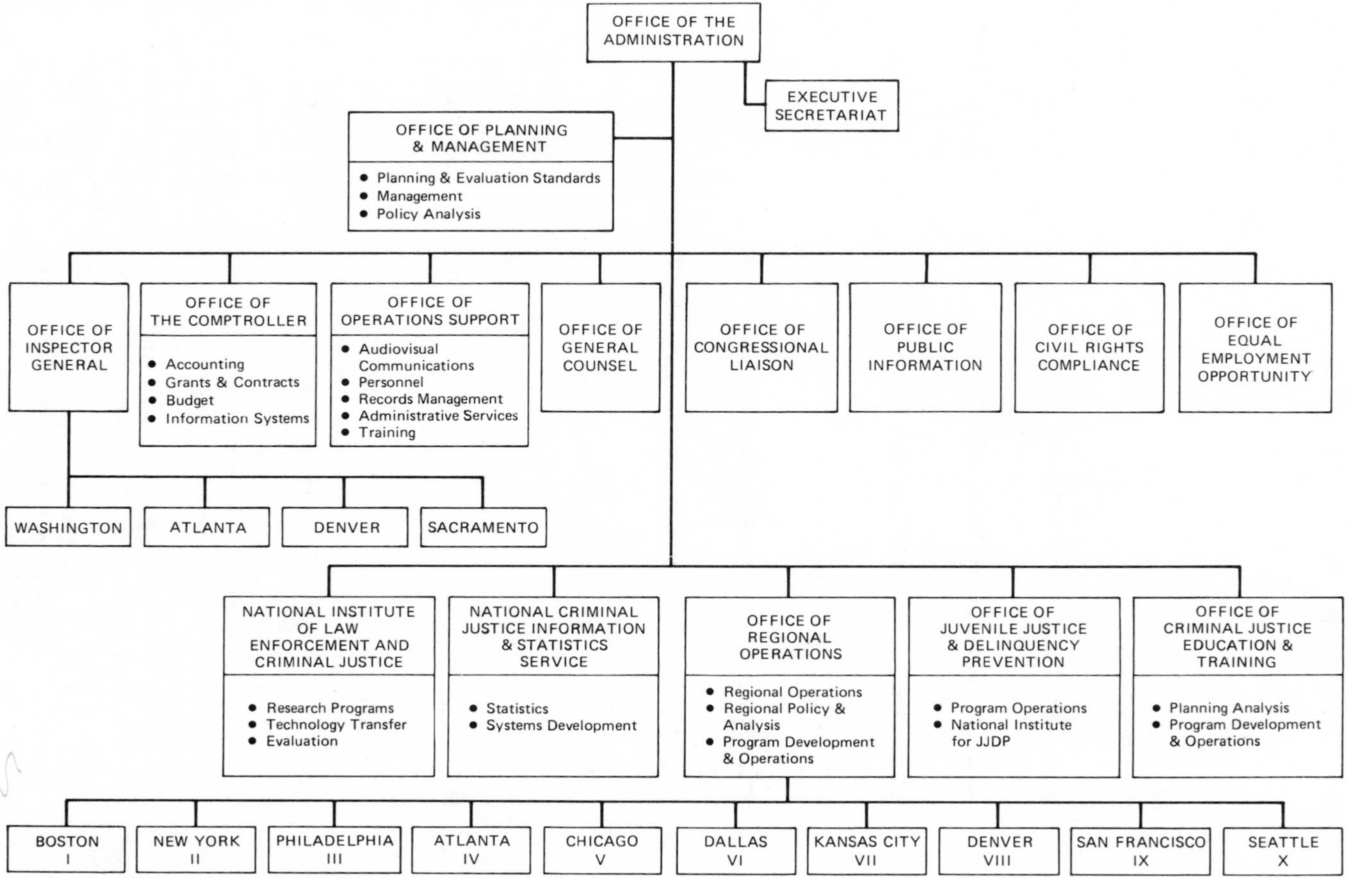

OFFICE OF THE ADMINISTRATION

EXECUTIVE SECRETARIAT

OFFICE OF INSPECTOR GENERAL

OFFICE OF PLANNING & MANAGEMENT
- Planning & Evaluation Standards
- Management
- Policy Analysis

OFFICE OF THE COMPTROLLER
- Accounting
- Grants & Contracts
- Budget
- Information Systems

OFFICE OF OPERATIONS SUPPORT
- Audiovisual
- Communications
- Personnel
- Records Management
- Administrative Services
- Training

OFFICE OF GENERAL COUNSEL

OFFICE OF CONGRESSIONAL LIAISON

OFFICE OF PUBLIC INFORMATION

OFFICE OF CIVIL RIGHTS COMPLIANCE

OFFICE OF EQUAL EMPLOYMENT OPPORTUNITY

NATIONAL INSTITUTE OF LAW ENFORCEMENT AND CRIMINAL JUSTICE
- Research Programs
- Technology Transfer
- Evaluation

NATIONAL CRIMINAL JUSTICE INFORMATION & STATISTICS SERVICE
- Statistics
- Systems Development

OFFICE OF REGIONAL OPERATIONS
- Regional Operations
- Regional Policy & Analysis
- Program Development & Operations

OFFICE OF JUVENILE JUSTICE & DELINQUENCY PREVENTION
- Program Operations
- National Institute for JJDP

OFFICE OF CRIMINAL JUSTICE EDUCATION & TRAINING
- Planning Analysis
- Program Development & Operations

WASHINGTON
ATLANTA
DENVER
SACRAMENTO

BOSTON I
NEW YORK II
PHILADELPHIA III
ATLANTA IV
CHICAGO V
DALLAS VI
KANSAS CITY VII
DENVER VIII
SAN FRANCISCO IX
SEATTLE X

FIGURE 1. LEAA organization chart

Source: Law Enforcement Assistance Administration.

FIGURE 2.   LEAA Budget History (in $ Millions)

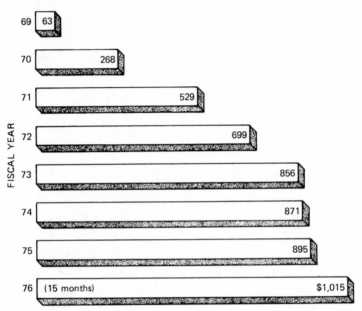

LEAA BUDGET HISTORY (in $ Millions)

FISCAL YEAR	
69	63
70	268
71	529
72	699
73	856
74	871
75	895
76 (15 months)	$1,015

Source: Law Enforcement Assistance Administration, *The Law Enforcement Assistance Administration: A Partnership for Crime Control* (Washington, D.C., 1976), p. 42.

"underdogs" is accomplished.[4] However, many criminologists who have relatively extensive relationships with LEAA would disagree strenuously with such bold assertions. LEAA is a complex and often

---

[4] Richard Quinney, *Critique of Legal Order* (Boston: Little, Brown, 1974), pp. 105–35. We have no quarrel with those assertions of Quinney and other radical criminologists in which it is argued that the legal system operates to protect dominant social and economic interests in modern societies. Speaking of LEAA, Quinney comments (p. 105): "The purpose of these agencies, and of the agents who constitute them, is the strengthening of the prevailing economic and political order." That observation and others made by Quinney are unexceptionable and patently obvious as well. The problem arises when Quinney begins to offer descriptions of LEAA that suggest the existence of a small, deliberate band of powerful conspirators behind such agencies as LEAA, who engage in malevolent schemes. For example, at one point (p. 109), Quinney states that "in the name of 'criminal justice,' the national government is providing a comprehensive, coordinated system of repression." Although Quinney may view the activities of LEAA as repressive, it is unlikely that the officials of that agency or those who created it see their acts in that same way. In our view, radical discussions of crime control measures and kindred matters are often

FIGURE 3.   The LEAA Dollar Fiscal Year 1976
                    $1 Billion *

THE LEAA DOLLAR FISCAL YEAR 1976 $1 BILLION*

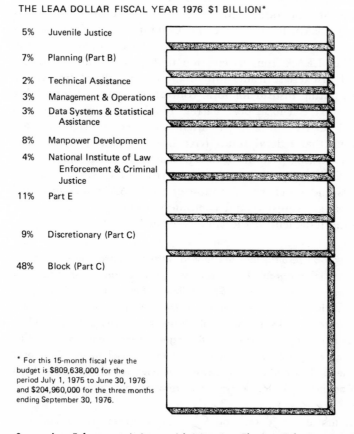

5%	Juvenile Justice
7%	Planning (Part B)
2%	Technical Assistance
3%	Management & Operations
3%	Data Systems & Statistical Assistance
8%	Manpower Development
4%	National Institute of Law Enforcement & Criminal Justice
11%	Part E
9%	Discretionary (Part C)
48%	Block (Part C)

* For this 15-month fiscal year the
budget is $809,638,000 for the
period July 1, 1975 to June 30, 1976
and $204,960,000 for the three months
ending September 30, 1976.

Source: Law Enforcement Assistance Administration, *The Law Enforcement Assistance Adminis-tration: A Partnership for Crime Control* (Washington, D.C., 1976), p. 43.

confused organization, pursuing a variety of not entirely coordinated goals and fulfilling various functions, some of which are manifest and others latent.

_____

filled with hyperbole, presenting an overly simplified characterization of the interests that are reflected in social policies, and flawed by gross hypotheses about "ruling class" conspiracies. The deficiencies of radical criminological thought are discussed at length in Don C. Gibbons, *Society, Crime, and Criminal Careers*, 3rd ed. (Engle-wood Cliffs, N.J.: Prentice-Hall, 1977), pp. 204–10. By contrast to radical views of LEAA, other critics of that agency have argued that it has failed to provide a com-prehensive, coordinated system of crime control!

There have been other criticisms of LEAA. Joseph Goulden has drawn attention to the early years of the agency, pointing out that most of the federal money was spent on tanks, helicopters, tear gas, radio equipment, and other military hardware.[5] Another salvo has been fired at LEAA by the Lawyers' Committee for Civil Rights under Law.[6] This group engaged in a searching examination of the performance of LEAA from its creation to 1972 and found that the agency failed to exercise leadership in influencing the states' use of block grants, opting instead for local control of funds and for LEAA money to be used as a local pork barrel. The lawyers' committee also blasted LEAA for its failure to pay attention to its civil rights obligations, charging that federal funds have been allocated to programs that reinforce existing patterns of discriminatory law enforcement and correctional decision making against minorities. The lawyers' group also echoed Goulden's charge that most of the LEAA money has gone to provide tear-gas canisters and computers, rather than for human services. In the judgment of the lawyers' committee:

> The over-all result is that the federal reform program has become a fiscal relief program. In almost four years of operation and after the distribution of roughly $1.5 billion in funds, the LEAA program has not initiated a basic reform of the nation's criminal justice system. Instead, LEAA has taken the system as given and invested its funds in making the criminal justice agencies more efficient, primarily through expenditures that meet existing material needs. This focus has tended to reinforce the present deficiencies of the criminal justice agencies, making fundamental reform more difficult.[7]

This matter of federal pork barrel programs is an endemic problem not confined to crime fighting. On this issue, David Stockman has drawn attention to the patterns of federal spending for social

---

[5] Joseph C. Goulden, "Feeding at the Federal Trough," in Isidore Silver, ed., *The Crime-Control Establishment* (Englewood Cliffs, N.J.: Prentice-Hall, 1974), pp. 138–49.

[6] Lawyers' Committee for Civil Rights under Law, *Law and Disorder III: State and Federal Performance under Title I of the Omnibus Crime Control and Safe Streets Act of 1968* (Washington, D.C., 1972). An even harsher report on the performance of LEAA was produced by the Lawyers' Committee in 1976. See Lawyers' Committee for Civil Rights under Law, *Law and Disorder IV: State and Federal Performance under Title I of the Omnibus Crime Control and Safe Streets Act of 1968* (Washington, D.C.: Center for National Security Studies, 1976).

[7] Lawyers' Committee, *Law and Disorder III*, p. 8.

welfare programs and contends that most of them have degenerated into a federal pork barrel, in which money is spent in ways that alleviate some of the financial difficulties of local jurisdictions, but which rarely have much effect upon the social problems they are supposed to address.[8] Welfare funding infrequently trickles down to the persons who were the focus of the original enabling legislation. For example, Stockman observes that the Hill-Burton Act, designed to meet the need for additional hospital facilities in this country, has been refunded to the point that we are now oversupplied with hospital beds! Federal spending on hospital construction meets some needs of the construction industry, but it has little to do with the health problems of the population, particularly those of low-income citizens who are more in need of access to adequate medical care than they are of hospitalization. Stockman draws the following conclusion regarding the pork barrel nature of federal funding:

> In short, the vast increase in federal social welfare outlays—from less than 6 percent of national income in 1950 to more than 15 percent today—has created in its wake a political maintenance system based in no small part on the cooptation and incorporation of Congress itself. If Members were ever legislators and statesmen, they have more and more taken on the characteristics of constituency ombudsmen and grant brokers. As a consequence, the aims of social policy have been subordinated to the exigencies of the new fiscal politics, and what may have been the bright promise of the Great Society has been transformed into a flabby hodge-podge, funded without policy consistency or rigor, that increasingly looks like a great social pork barrel.[9]

Although it is possible to draw an unflattering portrait of LEAA, much of the negative commentary regarding that agency seems unwarranted and exaggerated. Michael Serrill has produced an incisive, in-depth report on LEAA which is both critical and appreciative in tone.[10]

---

[8] David A. Stockman, "The Social Pork Barrel," *Public Interest,* 39 (Spring 1975), 3–30.

[9] Ibid., p. 13.

[10] Michael S. Serrill, "LEAA," *Corrections Magazine,* 2 (June 1976), 3–29; also see Law Enforcement Assistance Administration, *The Law Enforcement Assistance Administration: A Partnership for Crime Control* (Washington, D.C., 1976).

Serrill concedes that LEAA has not been without its problems and that it certainly has not suffered from a lack of critics in Congress and elsewhere. At the same time, he points out that seven different attorney generals supervised the agency during its first eight years. Even more important, LEAA has been directed by five different administrators since 1969, with an unworkable "troika" arrangement of three administrators in charge of the operation for part of that period. Serrill notes that this is a small agency as federal bureaucracies go, employing about 850 persons in all, with about 250 of them located in the ten regional offices of LEAA.

Serrill concedes that there is substance to complaints that LEAA has not maintained adequate control over funds allocated to the individual states, but he suggests that this failing is more attributable to the state justice planning agencies than to LEAA. However, a more fundamental point is that the total amount of money the agency has disbursed is quite meager, which is a comment we also offered in preceding pages. Serrill contends that it is unrealistic to expect the agency to have wrought miracles in the way of crime reduction, given the fact that its total yearly budget is only a small fraction of the amount being spent on police, courts, and corrections within the various states.

Serrill makes it quite clear that those criticisms of LEAA that have centered on funding of police armaments and so forth are at least somewhat outdated. He reports that the agency has also spent over $1.5 billion on correctional programs since 1969, and its current efforts are considerably more concentrated upon improving the workings of that part of the justice system than critics often concede. On this same point, he argues that LEAA funding has made possible many community-based treatment programs, diversion programs, training efforts, and drug-counseling activities that would not have developed without federal funding. LEAA funds underwrote the deinstitutionalization of juveniles from training schools in Massachusetts, an endeavor that we shall examine later in this chapter. Also, the Office of Juvenile Justice and Delinquency Prevention of LEAA has recently been involved in provision of funds for removal of status offenders from training schools, for diversion programs, and for other innovative ventures into juvenile corrections.

Serrill has some positive things to say about LEAA's efforts in the planning area, such as the agency's funding of the National Clearinghouse for Criminal Justice Planning and Architecture. LEAA has also provided the push for the development of comprehensive planning on the state level, which would probably not have come about without the efforts of this agency. Due to this pressure, justice planning operations have been created in all of the fifty states and in hundreds of local jurisdictions. It is this development with which we are most concerned.

FEDERAL LEGISLATION AND JUSTICE PLANNING

LEAA and Justice Planning

In the 1967 report of the President's Commission on Law Enforcement and Administration of Justice, a national strategy to reduce crime was proposed in which an attack upon the social and economic conditions associated with crime was to be guided by a total comprehensive plan and program. The commission made recommendations that would involve planning on both the federal and state levels. It envisioned the establishment of criminal justice planning agencies involving the three major subsystems of police, courts, and corrections in all the states and the use of federally funded grants-in-aid in order to support innovative state and local programs to reduce crime.

The Omnibus Crime Control and Safe Streets Act of 1968, which grew out of the earlier president's commission report, gave considerable impetus to the development of criminal justice planning and the emerging planner occupation-profession. More specifically, LEAA was authorized to provide funds to states that created state criminal justice planning agencies (SPAs). Eligibility for funds was to be determined on the basis of submission of an annual comprehensive plan, and funding was to be made on a block action grant basis. These block grants were to be used for direct law enforcement purposes encompassing all aspects of the criminal justice system, with smaller block planning grants awarded on a state basis to support the planning and grant administration efforts of the SPAs and their local or regional planning districts. The SPAs were to be administratively supervised by a board whose members represented state and local criminal justice agencies, citizen groups, and non–criminal justice public agencies. The board members have usually been appointed by the governor, and the director of the SPA is administratively responsible to him. Thus the comprehensive plan submitted by the SPA to LEAA for funding would usually move through the state policy supervisory board to the governor. The act also required that SPAs must be responsive to local government voices which are heard through the statewide policy boards and that 40 percent of all planning money allocated to the states be made available to local units. These local units, in turn, established regional or local planning councils with supervisory boards. Applications for project funds move through the local planning units to the SPAs.

Some sense of the original expectations of those who created the federal legislation and the planning mandate is captured by Daniel Skoler, writing at the time of the initial legislation. Skoler commented as follows regarding the 1968 federal crime legislation:

> A basic principle and mandate under all versions of the anticrime legislation now pending is that state and local governments must develop and maintain *comprehensive* improvement plans—that is, plans must consider all aspects of criminal administration: law enforcement, correction, courts and prosecution, citizen action, crime prevention. They must also integrate, to the greatest extent possible, the work of all agencies and levels of government carrying law enforcement and criminal justice responsibilities in the planning jurisdictions.[11]

By the end of 1975, every state and each of the territories, as well as the District of Columbia, had created state planning agencies. Five hundred regional, city, and county planning units had also been developed with federal, state, and local funds.[12] Currently about two thousand persons are involved in these planning agencies as criminal justice planners.

In theory, LEAA is responsible for setting the planning guidelines to be followed by the SPAs. The early years of federal funding were marked by emphasis on annual plans, while from 1973 to the present, more comprehensive multiyear planning based on standards and goals has been stressed by LEAA.

---

[11] Daniel L. Skoler, "Comprehensive Criminal Justice Planning—A New Challenge," *Crime and Delinquency*, 14 (July 1968), 197.

[12] Blair G. Ewing, "Criminal Justice Planning: An Assessment," *Criminal Justice Review*, 2 (Spring 1976), 121–39.

Evaluating the Planning Effort

How successful have these efforts to develop nationwide justice planning been? A reasoned judgment would be that federal involvement in crime fighting has not yet resulted in the development of mature, sophisticated justice planning. Much of the negative commentary has centered on the deficiencies of planning as practiced both by LEAA and at the state and regional levels. For example, the Lawyers' Committee for Civil Rights under Law examined the performance of LEAA from its creation to 1972 and concluded that the agency had failed to exercise leadership in influencing the states' use of block grants.[13] On the issue of planning, the lawyers' committee provided a detailed examination of state criminal justice planning operations that have developed as a part of the LEAA program. The committee report contains studies of criminal justice planning in California, Massachusetts, Ohio, Pennsylvania, and South Carolina. On the whole, the descriptions are not complimentary, for they indicate that much of what passes for planning is paper shuffling and that planning decisions are often highly partisan and political. Running throughout this report is the theme that LEAA money has been subjected to too much local control and has constituted a local pork barrel, so that federal funds have not been utilized in ways that have been identified through careful planning. In the words of the committee report:

> LEAA has not yet exercised the leadership mandated by Title I's design. It has not yet devoted sufficient attention and research effort to developing new tools for combatting crime or for measuring or understanding the problem of crime. Moreover, the federal agency has apparently chosen not to exercise strong leadership over the states in administering the block grants, and has not used the programs it administers directly to fill the gap . . . Generally, LEAA has neither led the way for the states, nor held the states up to strict performance standards. This has been as true of the operation and structure of the State Planning Agencies as of the quality

---

[13] Lawyers' Committee, *Law and Disorder III.* Also see Alan Kalmanoff, *Criminal Justice: Enforcement and Administration* (Boston: Little, Brown, 1976), pp. 11–12.

of state programming . . . Few of the states provide the technical assistance, leadership and program oversight for local programming that the Safe Streets Act intended them to provide. The overall result is that the federal program has become a fiscal relief program . . . This focus has tended to reinforce present deficiencies of the criminal justice agencies, making fundamental reform more difficult.[14]

Some parallel allegations have been offered by Michael Milakovich and Kurt Weiss, who argue that the war on crime has become politicized and has been perverted into a pork barrel for local jurisdictions.[15] These critics charge that LEAA officials do not know how the individual states are actually spending block money, having lost control of the distribution of that money. They indicate that a large portion of the money that in LEAA plans has been earmarked for training programs, attacks on crime causes, or preventive programs has been reallocated by the individual state planning agencies to the purchase of more lethal equipment by local police. Additionally, they claim that "although many states have produced impressive plans for the allocation of federal money according to the expressed needs of local criminal justice agencies, few have been able to put them into practice." [16]

The thrust of remarks to this point is that comprehensive criminal justice planning efforts at the national, state, and local levels have been frustrated by the intrusion of local politics and agency self-interests into decision making and expenditure of funds. Further, the extensive criminal justice planning mechanism outlined in the Safe Streets Act and subsequently established under LEAA direction at the state and regional levels has failed to emerge as the pivotal ingredient in the resource allocation process, which was envisioned as at least one of its key roles by the National Advisory Commission on Criminal Justice Standards and Goals.[17] This situation is quite similar to one

---

[14] Lawyers' Committee, Law and Disorder III, pp. 7–8.

[15] Michael E. Milakovich and Kurt Weiss, "Politics and Measures of Success in the War on Crime," Crime and Delinquency, 21 (January 1975), 1–10.

[16] Ibid., p. 8.

[17] National Advisory Commission on Criminal Justice Standards and Goals, Report on the Criminal Justice System (Washington, D.C.: Government Printing Office, 1973).

that has often been encountered in city planning, in which the informed and sophisticated land-use planning efforts of city planning agency technical staffs have been frustrated by zoning commissions or city officials responding to narrower self-interest appeals of businessmen, developers, and kindred individuals interested in maintaining the status quo.

However, rather than indicting totally the federal, state, and regional planning experience, it should be recognized that the planning process undertaken by LEAA in 1968 almost inevitably had to be developmental—that is, it gained sophistication with experience rather than beginning at full maturity. In his excellent summary of the evolution of the planning process under LEAA, Blair Ewing, director of the Division of Planning and Evaluation of LEAA, commented as follows:

> The progress made in the last seven years since the enactment of the Safe Streets Act is impressive, especially in the institutional sense. There is now in place a set of institutions charged with the responsibility for planning for law enforcement and criminal justice systems throughout the nation at regional, state and local levels. These agencies and their planning activities are sufficiently visible to criminal justice officials and to state and local government officials to assure that the concept of comprehensive planning for law enforcement and criminal justice has become, at least in general terms, familiar to them. State comprehensive plans have improved in quality over time. The planning process has drawn citizens, elected officials, and criminal justice officials together, often for the first time, and forced them to recognize and to address some, if perhaps not all, of the issues of interrelationships of agency activities at the local level, and the issues of relationships of Federal, state, city, and county roles in criminal justice. The planning process, even if imperfect, has frequently resulted in improved cooperation, better understanding among agencies, greater efficiency in operations, and a promise of greater effectiveness in fighting crime in the future. These results have not always been uniformly achieved, nor has the process always been harmonious. While amicable discussion and agreement have been usually the rule, there are a number of occasions on which bruising battles accompanied by open hostilities have occurred. If progress has not been as rapid or as accompanied by harmony as some had hoped, progress has been real enough nevertheless. The intention of those who drafted the Safe Streets Act that there should be comprehensive planning for the law

enforcement and criminal justice system of the nation is beginning to be realized.

Since nothing of the kind can be said to have existed prior to 1965, the progress made is considerable. The development of an understanding of the methods for accomplishing comprehensive planning has been gradual, with understanding increasing as experience with the problems and implementation of successful planning in this arena is an evolutionary process.

If we have come some distance in the past decade, we still have a considerable distance to go. Three years and four sets of plans ago, the National Advisory Commission on Criminal Justice Standards and Goals offered its view of the state of comprehensive planning in law enforcement and criminal justice, based on its examination of those first four sets of plans. The Commission noted four major deficiencies in the plans and in the process that produced them. These were: (1) the narrow scope of the plans, which meant that they appeared to focus almost exclusively on the expenditure of the Federal funds available from LEAA, which constituted typically only 5 to 10 per cent of all criminal justice expenditures; (2) a lack of reliable data and statistics which could clearly define the nature, scope, and trends in crime, and the nature and scope of the criminal justice system's problems in dealing with crime; (3) a lack of precise statements about goals, directions, and strategies for addressing crime and criminal justice problems; and (4) a lack of systematic efforts to measure performance and a lack of methods which would permit the use of performance measurement results in future plans and programs. This judgment was surely accurate when it was offered in January, 1973.

These deficiencies, in lesser measure, continue to exist today, three years and four sets of plans later.[18]

In his essay, Ewing moves on to identify some of the major sources or causes of the deficiencies that continue to plague efforts at comprehensive criminal justice planning. He enumerates four major problems: the fragmentation or the nonsystem character of the criminal justice apparatus, the narrow definition of planning that grew out of the Safe Streets Act which has led to a constricted view of the planning function, insufficient attention to the data and informational

---

[18] Ewing, "Criminal Justice Planning," pp. 123–24.

needs upon which informed planning might proceed, and uncertainty about the most viable planning approaches for comprehensive, systemwide criminal justice and law enforcement planning.

The nonsystem character of the criminal justice machinery has been alluded to in Chapter 1, and we shall return to a detailed consideration of some of the interorganizational conflicts and other indications of system fragmentation in Chapter 3. But at this point we should acknowledge the validity of Ewing's major point that because the criminal justice system is not managed from a single location within the system or under the aegis of a single branch of government, comprehensive planning for the entire system is made exceedingly difficult to accomplish.

Ewing argues that many planners have reacted to the fragmentation of the system by avoiding attention to systemwide planning, opting instead for a narrower definition of planning focused on specific agencies and their problems. He avers that LEAA enabling legislation and LEAA policies in the early years of this agency contributed to this narrowing of the planning focus. LEAA guidelines have been modified in the light of the Crime Control Act of 1973 to stress comprehensive planning, but "the earlier narrower interpretation of the focus of the comprehensive plan was a barrier to the development of comprehensive planning for the entire criminal justice system, because it discouraged planners from attempting broader planning, and justified them in their decision to spend little time on planning." [19] Ewing concedes that the result of the processes that evolved at the state and local levels for disbursing federal funds is a form of financial pie-cutting or pork barrel.[20]

Ewing's discussion also draws attention to the absence of reliable criminal justice data, which has frustrated planning efforts in the past. However, he also points out that there has recently been a data explosion, so that the planner's dilemma has shifted to the question of how to manage and analyze the vast quantity of information now at hand. Chapter 7 of this book speaks to that issue at greater length.[21]

---

[19] Ibid., p. 127.

[20] Ibid., p. 128.

[21] One LEAA response to the problem of data management and data analysis is the monograph published by that agency on quantitative skills for planners. See Leonard Oberlander, ed., *Quantitative Tools for Criminal Justice Planning* (Washington, D.C.: Law Enforcement Assistance Administration, 1975).

Ewing devotes considerable space in his analysis to the uncertainty and disagreement about the most promising and appropriate models to be used in justice planning. By and large, this uncertainty is related to some other developments in justice planning that he pinpointed. Additionally, Ewing is in agreement with a major thesis of this book, namely, that criminal justice planning is a budding profession at best, lacking a comprehensive body of theory, knowledge, and skills which would provide the undergirding of a criminal justice planning profession.

Ewing's observations end on a relatively optimistic note. He suggests that there is some emerging consensus among justice planners to the effect that incrementalist or process models hold greater promise for justice planning than do blueprinting or the construction of master plans, on the one hand, or a heavily research-oriented focus, on the other. Briefly described, *incremental planning* centers on the development of increasingly more rational and comprehensive justice plans through successive approximations in which plans are formulated and then implemented, with feedback on their effectiveness being produced by research, which then leads to revisions in the plan. We shall return to some further examination of these three planning models in Chapter 3.

Ewing also offers some observations about new methodological techniques now available to planners, through which incremental planning can be aided. He also draws attention to some recent trends in the direction of greater interest on the part of SPAs in systemwide planning. Finally, he points out that recent LEAA efforts in the direction of training of planners in justice system planning, crime analysis, and program evaluation augur well for progress in the direction of growing sophistication of justice planning. He concludes with the following comments:

> It is essential that progress be made toward mastery of these problems, since there is still a strong belief, embedded in the Act which governs the LEAA program, that good planning necessarily precedes effective action to improve the criminal justice system and reduce crime. Some important steps forward have been taken since January, 1973, when the National Advisory Commission pointed out major deficiencies in planning in the program. While these deficiencies have not been eliminated, and while many of them now appear to be inherent elements of the criminal justice system itself, it is possible to attack them and to develop strategies for improving the

performance of criminal justice planning. And that has been in fact
the history of the past three years.[22]

One other positive development, not reported by Ewing, is the
LEAA funding of the National Clearinghouse for Criminal Justice
Planning and Architecture at the University of Illinois, which offers a
broad variety of technical assistance services to state and local criminal
justice agencies, planners, architects, and others in a concerted effort
to improve the performance of the criminal justice system. The national clearinghouse has developed survey instruments, data analysis
techniques, and program linkage methods to be used in formulating
"master" plans for state and local criminal justice programs. For the
most part the national clearinghouse incorporates current program
knowledge into its study-consultation efforts and applies this information to assessment of state and community criminal justice programs
in the form of recommendations for system improvements. Recommendations flowing from master plans developed by the national
clearinghouse are then turned over to local and state governments for
funding and implementation.

The national clearinghouse's program is noteworthy in that it
has given a strong boost to information-based planning. To a large
degree, the national clearinghouse has captured the study-consultation
role long played by the National Council on Crime and Delinquency.
However, with its considerably larger staff and with nationwide LEAA
support of criminal justice programs, it has been possible for the
clearinghouse to focus to a greater extent on system relationships. The
importance of this activity should not be understated, since it applies
a much needed systemwide approach to the criminal justice field to
replace the spotty and fragmented efforts that have characterized the
criminal justice enterprise in the past.

CURRENT PLANNING: SOME EXAMPLES

We have spoken generally about the development of justice planning
in the United States and of the shortcomings of that activity to date.
Let us now turn to a more detailed examination of the planning ex-

---

22 Ewing, "Criminal Justice Planning," p. 139.

perience as it has unfolded in some specific instances. These illustrative cases are offered so that some life can be breathed into the generalizations offered in preceding sections of this chapter.

The Oregon State Planning Experience

Let us begin with a fairly detailed discussion of state planning in Oregon since the creation of LEAA. This is a case with which we are quite familiar. More important, the Oregon experience of halting progress toward planning maturity is probably representative of developments in many other states as well.[23] The Oregon account provides some more up-to-date observations on planning under LEAA, to supplement those of the Lawyers' Committee on Civil Rights under Law, which followed developments in five states only to 1972. Significant progress has been made since then, at least in Oregon.

EARLY DEVELOPMENTS.   The Oregon Law Enforcement Council was created by legislative action in 1969 to replace the Oregon Crime Control Coordinating Council that was established in 1967. The predecessor organization was an outgrowth of the longtime interest of the then attorney general, Robert Thornton, in developing a state-level criminal justice planning and coordinating mechanism in the attorney general's office to deal more effectively with the fragmented, disparate state and local criminal justice nonsystem then existing. This initial legislation placed major responsibility for undertaking criminal justice coordinating activities in the State Corrections Division.

During the two-year history of the Crime Control Coordinating Council, the Corrections Division developed and obtained the initial federal planning grant from the federal Office of Law Enforcement Assistance. Through the planning grant, a small staff was organized to prepare the foundation for the broader planning mechansim

---

[23] Oregon was one of five states selected by LEAA for intensive case studies of the development of criminal justice standards and goals. See Law Enforcement Assistance Administration, *Criminal Justice Standards and Goals for Oregon: A Case Study* (Washington, D.C., 1975). The other four states studied by LEAA were Michigan, Florida, Utah, and Texas. The report on Oregon contains a number of suggestions and recommendations regarding ways that states might more productively go about developing goals, standards, and comprehensive plans.

that was to be required under the pending Omnibus Crime Control and Safe Streets Act. The staff also undertook revisions of the coordinating council legislation to bring it into conformity with the federal act. The 1969 Oregon legislature changed the designation of the policy body from the Crime Control Coordinating Council to the Oregon Law Enforcement Council (OLEC) and expunged the provisions identifying the governor as chairman and the attorney general as vice-chairman of the council.

The present Oregon statute governing the functions and responsibilities of OLEC and the appointed administrator remains substantially the same as the original 1967 act. OLEC is responsible for planning, developing, and carrying out a long-range statewide crime and delinquency control and prevention program. The statutory provisions also indicate that the council will assist local communities in planning and development, and in addition that the council will serve as a supervisory body for law enforcement and for juvenile delinquency planning programs initiated by federal legislation. This statutory provision gives the council clear authority to approve, disapprove, or modify planning and programs presented to OLEC for block or discretionary funding by state or local agencies.

The statute defines specifically the responsibilities of the administrator of OLEC, including supervision of all matters relating to the crime control and prevention program, development of an information system, and authority to conduct surveys and studies into the causes of crime and delinquency. The statute also sets forth a clear mandate for the OLEC administrator to establish local law enforcement planning-coordinating mechanisms. Finally, the statute gives the administrator responsibility for establishing similar councils in local schools, but this task appears to have been included in the law as a statement of an ideal rather than a realistic goal.

The original Law Enforcement Council consisted of twenty-two members of state and local criminal justice agencies and representatives of the community-at-large, along with a planning staff of six persons. The new agency interpreted its administrative functions as primarily those of preparing the state's comprehensive plan, establishing priorities for action and funding as part of the plan, and providing fiscal and program monitoring. Other functions included encouragement of regional and metropolitan planning efforts and, most importantly, "oversight and evaluation of the total State effort in plan implementation and law enforcement improvement."

The first step taken by the council in 1968–69 focused on

organization of local planning units as provided in the federal act. In the first months of the agency's existence, formal organizations were established in all fourteen of the state's administrative districts. In six of the administrative districts, COGs (Councils of Government) were designated as the district law enforcement planning agencies, while the eight remaining districts formed law enforcement planning committees which in turn were officially designated as district law enforcement planning agencies.

The second step taken by the new state planning organization was to obtain from state and local groups an identification of projects for needed criminal justice system improvements. Within a matter of weeks, a compendium of projected needs totaling just over $42 million was assembled and communicated to the federal Law Enforcement Assistance Administration! The final step was the distribution of the initial federal action fund allocation of $245,514 to state and local criminal justice agencies.

The meager amount of federal money available in the first year of the program and the adopted priorities led to commitment of the largest amount of funds to a criminal justice information system and to the prevention and control of riots and civil disorders. The latter had been given special emphasis a few months earlier by LEAA, with a special grant to all states following the general unrest that had flared up in urban areas in 1967 and 1968. Lesser amounts were allocated to correctional facilities and programs, public education and information, law enforcement–community relations, and court functions, in that order.

Oregon represents a case in point of the funding and planning pattern identified by Ewing, Milakovich and Weiss, and other critics of the federal crime-fighting effort. This initial focus on funding priorities, in conjunction with the emphasis upon state disbursement to local governmental units, set a pattern resembling revenue sharing rather than comprehensive planning. The local units were anxious from the outset of the Safe Streets program to obtain their "fair share" of the federal funds without particular attention to the nature, scope, and demographic character of the statewide crime problem. Once this pattern was established, efforts on the part of the State Planning Agency to provide leadership and direction based upon more intensive study and planning resulted in the continuing political tug of war to maintain the status quo that is apparent even now. Not all of the local planning units were interested solely in receipt of federal funds without direction and guidelines from the state; nonetheless, OLEC has had difficulty over the years in its attempts to restructure the priority funding formula in line with a comprehensive planning design.[24]

THE STATE PLANNING AGENCY.   Administration of the federal funding is the responsibility of the State Planning Agency (SPA), consisting of the Oregon Law Enforcement Council (OLEC) and its approximately thirty-seven full-time employees. The council, appointed by the governor, currently has a membership of twenty-one members, ranging from representatives of the criminal justice system (sheriffs, city police, district attorneys, adult and juvenile court judges) to locally elected governmental officials and private citizens. The current structure of the planning enterprise in Oregon is shown in Figure 4.

OLEC's stated purpose is "to be a catalyst in the reduction of crime in Oregon by assisting state agencies and units of local government in strengthening and improving law enforcement and criminal justice at every level." The chairman of OLEC is appointed by the governor, and the chairman in turn appoints the vice-chairman. The

---

[24] Shortly after the passage of the federal Safe Streets legislation, the Congress also enacted the Juvenile Delinquency Prevention and Control Act of 1968, and in Oregon responsibility for the administration of this act was assigned by the governor to the Law Enforcement Council. The new delinquency legislation was drastically underfunded, and the federal Youth Development and Delinquency Prevention Administration (YDDPA), located within the Department of Health, Education, and Welfare, focused its efforts broadly on three specific subject areas: (1) defining a role for youth in society, (2) diversion of children from the juvenile justice system, and (3) improvement of youth-adult relations. In 1971 YDDPA and LEAA agreed to a separation of activity areas, with YDDPA focusing on prevention and diversion and LEAA confining its attention to functions related to children entering the juvenile justice system.

Oregon received its first delinquency prevention planning grant in late 1969 and by June 1970 had completed a general planning document. This document was expanded in the second year of the planning period, but funds for the third year were frozen by YDDPA because the Oregon plan did not meet federal requirements. This matter remained in limbo until 1974 when the money was released to the Oregon Children's Services Division to use for the development of a data system for tracking children placed by the juvenile courts in out-of-home care.

A point worth noting in the history of the Juvenile Delinquency and Prevention Control Act of 1968 is that there was much resistance at the congressional level to this bill, centered on the amount of federal money spent in the early 1960s by the Office of Juvenile Delinquency and Youth Development, the predecessor organization to YDDPA, and the questionable results of these programs. In any event, YDDPA received minimal funding under the 1968 act and played a secondary role to LEAA in the funding of delinquency projects. The YDDPA has now been replaced by a new federal administrative structure under the Juvenile Justice and Delinquency Prevention Act of 1974, funded and administered under LEAA.

FIGURE 4. Oregon Criminal Justice Planning Structure

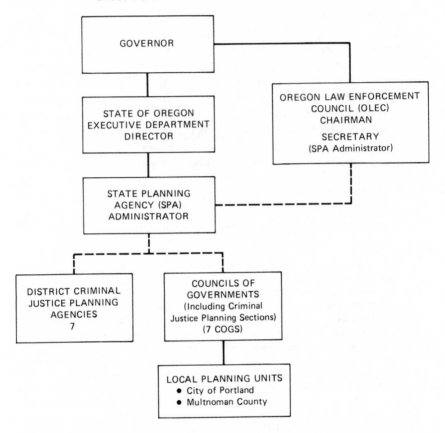

OREGON CRIMINAL JUSTICE PLANNING STRUCTURE

Source: Law Enforcement Assistance Administration, *Criminal Justice Standards and Goals for Oregon: A Case Study* (Washington, D.C., 1975).

council itself meets at least on a quarterly basis, but the various council committees may meet more frequently. The council's structure also includes plan development committees (PDCs), which function in the areas of corrections, law enforcement, courts, juvenile, and information systems. An executive committee consisting of the council chairman and the respective chairmen of the PDCs has broad authority to function as an interim policy body between the council's regularly scheduled meetings. The executive committee takes action on administrative issues with policy implications as well as on routine council business. It also has the authority to review action grant proposals from state and local planning agencies and to supervise and coordinate implementation of various council programs relating to the state comprehensive plan and action programs. Clearly, the council has given the executive committee far-reaching authority.

REGIONAL PLANNING UNITS.   As noted previously, the predecessor organization to the Law Enforcement Council moved immediately in 1967 to establish planning entities in each of the state's fourteen administrative districts. Combinations of Councils of Government (COGs) and technical advisory committees (TACs) were created and designated as regional planning units. The technical advisory committee functions include the provision of expertise in criminal justice planning to local COGs, supervision or oversight of the local district's participation in state council programs, and accountability to the local COGs, or political decision makers for criminal justice programs. Currently, each of the administrative districts also has a full- or part-time planning staff responsible for development and coordination of the local criminal justice planning effort.

PROGRESS TO DATE.   Planning and fund distribution has proceeded through a number of stages since the development of the state criminal justice mechanism in 1967. As indicated above, early emphasis was given to organizing both state and district planning bodies to meet LEAA requirements and provide the structure for distribution of federal funds. Broad directions were provided by the SPA in assisting state and local agencies in developing priorities, but in the first year or two of the program, the planning-fund distribution process lacked organization and precision. Over the years, however, the total process has improved measurably. Both OLEC and the local districts have developed planning capabilities that have permitted these agencies to commit themselves to annual and multiyear planning. The more recent thrust, flowing from the recommendations of the National Advisory Commission on Criminal Justice Standards and Goals in 1973, establishes a specific goal-oriented focus to state and district planning that was considerably more vague in the earlier years of the program.

On the other hand, one might expect that OLEC and district planning entities would eventually have achieved a mutually acceptable *modus operandi* in planning, policymaking, and funding. The elements for a relatively sophisticated interdependent process have evolved since the program's inception in 1967, and yet as late as 1976, it was quite obvious that the organizational network was still plagued by vestiges of difficulties dating back to earlier years but now institutionalized. A number of examples of these difficulties will illustrate the point.

There now exists at both the OLEC and district levels a general commitment to a planning process. Recruitment of planners, particularly at the state level, has emphasized employment of individuals with field experience in one or another criminal justice component and with experience in or at least exposure to the planning process. Planners at the local level have been recruited primarily from criminal justice line agencies, particularly law enforcement and corrections. Both state and local planners have had the opportunity to participate in a course given at the Criminal Justice Planning Institute, conducted by the Center for Administration of Justice, University of Southern California, and sponsored by LEAA. This course has provided staff members with an introduction to planning theory and practice and has included an orientation to tactical and strategic planning, goal-oriented planning, and monitoring and evaluation.

However, despite the many efforts to establish a common approach to comprehensive planning through goal identification and priorities selection, "projecting" continues to dominate the planning process. OLEC planners often express frustration arising from their perception that the SPA is simply viewed by the districts as a funding mechanism to underwrite district criminal justice program needs. Local district planners and their advisory and policy boards are equally reactive to any indications that the OLEC policy group or staff are inclined to dictate local planning or implementation strategies. The entire planning scene then remains something of a "standoff," awaiting intervention from some source or another that might push the system into action and toward the task of comprehensive criminal justice planning.

There is an obvious historical explanation for this situation. Without clear guidelines in the first year or two of the program, and with federal funds in increasing amounts available, state and local criminal justice agencies simply took advantage of the opportunity to expand existing programs or to undertake often-denied programs. The budgetary circumstances of state and local criminal justice agencies have deteriorated even more since the early years of the program, with state and local governments caught between inflation and increasing demands and having to strain even to maintain existing services. Under these circumstances, when "survival" dominates the thinking of most governmental agencies, planning takes on the trappings of an ideal rather than being a realistic and necessary alternative to maintaining an existing service level.

A second difficulty in the OLEC program is the role played by the policymaking bodies at state and local levels. Members of such groups, including criminal justice representatives, politicians, and citizens-at-large, come to the policy forum with their own sets of values and preferences. Ideally, sound policy decisions should stem from prior planning that provides policymakers with a perspective on issues which permits them to negotiate and arrive at reasonable consensus for action. A shared perspective is critical to the policymaking process, so that policymakers must have a clear understanding of both their role as policy board members and the function of their policy body as set forth in statute and/or organization bylaws. Lacking a clear perspective on these roles, the policymaking degenerates into narrow expression of personal bias or constituency needs to the detriment of system goals.

To a greater or lesser extent, this state of affairs characterizes policymaking at the OLEC and district levels. Planning as a design process for setting forth criminal justice system goals is often given only lip service by OLEC and district decision-making groups. At the OLEC level specifically, council members have the strongest commitment to their local area or professional constituencies, resulting in the continued reinforcement of project funding. A similar condition appears to exist at the district level where local planning is directed by TACs and COGs, rather than these groups meshing their decisions within the context of an overall system planning design. Underlying the problem at both OLEC and district levels is a fundamental lack of understanding of the urgency of planning and the importance of aligning the policy decision-making process to the planning design.

The other side of the coin is that there are encouraging signs for the future in the Oregon planning arrangement, for the difficulties of years past are clearly seen by a number of district and state law enforcement policy body members and a variety of plans have been proposed to improve the entire statewide planning mechanism. Most recently, a strong commitment has been given to continuation of the local planning thrust, even in predominantly rural districts where questions have frequently been raised as to the need for planning staff. Efforts are also under way to assess and define the roles and relationships of state and district planning staff, holding promise that the inevitable tug-of-war between state and local planning bodies may be clarified and structured to mitigate in the future the animosity and competition that dilutes the effectiveness of total planning efforts. Finally, the Oregon Law Enforcement Council policy board appears to be coming to grips with its own function as the state-level policy body, developing a clearer fix on its role in determining the direction and thrust of criminal justice programs in Oregon and moving away from an almost continual involvement in "grants review," a longtime nagging irritant to local planning bodies. The future shape and form of state and local planning functions and relationships can be seen only in broad outline at this point, but it is clear that the planning process in Oregon is maturing and future planning and programming in the criminal justice system should reflect this "coming of age."

The Massachusetts Experience in Deinstitutionalization

The Massachusetts program change toward deinstitutionalization of juvenile offenders represents a situation involving radical correctional reform, in contrast to the slower crescive and evolutionary approach taken in many other states to de-emphasize incarceration of juvenile offenders. After being appointed administrator of the state Department of Youth Services, Jerome Miller first endeavored to introduce rehabilitation programs within the ten state institutions for juvenile offenders. Miller's efforts included termination of such practices as shaving the heads of wards and other barbarisms, but his most important actions centered on restructuring the training schools in the direction of therapeutic communities. However, Miller's institutional reform efforts were not only plagued by inadequate financing and kindred impediments but vigorously and bitterly resisted by many of the staff members in these institutions.

After experiencing repeated frustration in these reform efforts, Director Miller in 1971–72 initiated a major effort to close the state juvenile facilities and to provide community-based program alternatives to them. The history of this process of deinstitutionalization has been described in detail by Ohlin, Coates, and Miller [25] and by Bakal.[26]

The particular methodology employed by Miller is instructive in the study of planning perspectives. Several key factors were in-

---

[25] Lloyd E. Ohlin, Robert D. Coates, and Alden D. Miller, "Radical Correctional Reform: A Case Study of the Massachusetts Youth Correctional System," *Harvard Educational Review,* 44 (February 1974), 74–111. Another case of planned deinstitutionalization, involving the Windsor, Vermont, state prison, is reported in Cornelius D. Hogan and William R. Steinhurst, "Managing Change in Corrections," *Federal Probation,* 40 (June 1976), 55–59.

[26] Yitzhak Bakal, "Closing Massachusetts' Institutions: A Case Study," in Bakal, ed., *Closing Correctional Institutions* (Lexington, Mass.: Lexington Books, 1973).

volved in the implementation of his radical approach within a relatively short period of time. From the outset he had key support at the highest political level in the state, as well as from various citizen and professional groups who agreed with his basic position that incarceration was a destructive experience for youth and that a more constructive treatment experience could be provided in community-based facilities. The climate was ripe for change because of the controversy surrounding the state's juvenile institutions in the late 1960s. The availability of LEAA funds provided Miller with the necessary resources with which to develop alternative treatment programs. These funds enabled him to hire top staff committed to his philosophy of change, circumventing the restrictions of the civil service system. The funds also allowed him to establish new types of community-based treatment services and supportive educational, recreational, and training services in these agencies.

While Miller's approach to changing the juvenile correctional scene in Massachusetts was a flexible one, dealing with issues as they emerged, he did establish a plan based upon available sociological theory which stresses the lack of positive effects from institutional treatment. A unit of planners, in cooperation with key departmental administrators, produced a seven-point plan which set the pattern for reform. This plan called for regionalization, community-based treatment centers, expansion of the forestry camp program, relocation of detention facilities, increased placement alternatives, grants-in-aid to cities and towns, and an intensive care security unit. While the planning unit and top administrativbe staff were caught up in recurrent crises, they also continued to procure federal funds to implement their plan. It is doubtful that without LEAA funds the transition from the training school structure to noninstitutional alternatives would have been achieved so rapidly.

The key planning question in the Massachusetts experience is whether the same innovations could have been accomplished successfully with a more gradual approach. It is clear that as long as Miller had key support at the highest political level, he was able to continue a program of reform and innovation. Such support, however, is inevitably built on a shifting base and can deteriorate rapidly when constituency reaction begins to form in opposition to the changes. Further, a radical change strategy almost inevitably produces some alienation between administration and staff persons that is detrimental to organizational stability. Perhaps even more critical to a radical change strategy is the support of the key actors in the criminal justice field at the grass-roots level, namely, judges, law enforcement officials, and probation officers. A change strategy may have support at the state executive and legislative levels, and even among state- and local-level citizen and professional groups, but it will become vulnerable if support cannot also be maintained from key local criminal justice officials. The latter represent an important political constituency whose views may ultimately serve to undermine the support a change-oriented administration has at both the executive and legislative levels. This actually occurred in Massachusetts where many judges, law enforcement officials, and probation officers, including many of those initially sympathetic to the idea of reform, began to oppose the new administration, resulting eventually in legislative investigations of reforms.[27]

The Massachusetts reform program is deserving of more critical analysis as a case study than it can receive in this book. What can be said about the experience, however, is that the change process was largely ad hoc in concept and implementation. Although the basic thesis of deinstitutionalization was accepted by many, the implementation process set up reverberations that resulted in continual turmoil. In retrospect, the Massachusetts reform effort can be viewed as more of a social movement than as a longitudinal planning process incorporating a step-by-step building of support on the part of interest groups, attenuation of ideological polarization, and goal clarification leading to consensus on tactics and strategies of change. The Massachusetts reform approach provides a commentary on the state of criminal justice planning today. Major changes were seen as critical and were attacked frontally. In the long run, the criminal justice system must develop a planning structure that will make such radical reform measures increasingly less necessary. The Massachusetts reform effort may ultimately make its greatest contribution by focusing increased attention upon planning theory and methodology in the future.

Federal Funding of Juvenile Diversion

A final experience which involved relatively coherent and comprehensive planning can be offered, dealing with the federally funded program of diversion of youths out of the official juvenile

---

[27] Ohlin, Coates, and Miller, "Radical Correctional Reform." Serrill has presented a series of four articles dealing in detail with the Massachusetts experience. See Michael S. Serrill, "Juvenile Corrections in Massachusetts," "Harvard Recidivism Study," "Moving the Kids Out: A Unique Experience," and "Jerome Miller: Does He Have the Answers to Juvenile Corrections?", Corrections Magazine, 2 (November-December 1975), 3–40.

justice system. The general movement toward diversion has grown out of various sources: the overload of cases in the juvenile court, labeling theory in the sociological study of deviance, and recent developments in delinquency theory and research.[28] For example, a number of deviance theorists have concluded that the juvenile court is often a stigmatizing experience that drives youngsters further into deviant careers rather than impelling them out of misconduct. Accordingly, a number of persons have offered advice similar to that proffered by sociologist Edwin Schur: "Thus, the basic injunction for public policy becomes: *leave kids alone whenever possible*" (emphasis in original).[29]

However, although juvenile diversion is a plausible notion and is also one of those faddish proposals that has many supporters, relatively little hard evidence can be mustered to demonstrate that diversion of juveniles to alternative programs outside the juvenile court is any more beneficial than either court referral or outright release of youths from the justice system.[30] In short, diversion is one of those popular reform proposals that cries out for more experimentation and research testing.

The Office of Juvenile Justice and Delinquency Prevention of LEAA, established through the Juvenile Justice and Delinquency Prevention Act of 1974, embarked in 1975 on a planning effort leading to the funding of a series of diversion projects throughout the United States. This federal agency allocated $10 million to this diversion effort, from which it was hoped that some answers to key questions about diversion would ultimately be provided.

The Office of Juvenile Justice and Delinquency Prevention engaged two of the authors of this book to assist in the planning effort. Those authors and additional persons employed through a planning and evaluation grant awarded to Portland State University collaborated

---

[28] The arguments for juvenile diversion are outlined in Law Enforcement Assistance Administration, *Program Announcement: Diversion of Youth from the Juvenile Justice System* (Washington, D.C.: Office of Juvenile Justice and Delinquency Prevention, April 1976). Also see Don C. Gibbons, *Delinquent Behavior*, 2nd ed. (Englewood Cliffs, N.J.: Prentice-Hall, 1976), pp. 260–67; and Robert M. Carter and Malcolm W. Klein, eds., *Back on the Street: The Diversion of Juvenile Offenders* (Englewood Cliffs, N.J.: Prentice-Hall, 1976).

[29] Edwin M. Schur, *Radical Non-Intervention* (Englewood Cliffs, N.J.: Prentice-Hall, 1973), p. 155.

[30] Don C. Gibbons and Gerald F. Blake, "Evaluating the Impact of Juvenile Diversion Programs," *Crime and Delinquency*, 22 (October 1976), 411–20. The reader might be advised to examine the entire collection of papers in this special issue of *Crime and Delinquency*: "Diversion in the Juvenile Justice System."

in the diversion planning process with the special emphasis program staff in the Office of Juvenile Justice.

The planning process itself unfolded along the following lines. First, a number of meetings were held in Washington, D.C., between the Office of Juvenile Justice planners, the Portland State University consultants, and outside experts on various dimensions of the diversion issue. These meetings were designed to identify the major issues that need to be confronted in diversion, including due-process protections for diverted youth and the thorny question of the kind of program model or models to be funded. To date a wide variety of diversion endeavors have resulted, centered on a number of different orientations to juvenile misconduct and appropriate intervention strategies. Some existing programs are based on psychogenic images of offenders, holding that they are troubled youths who need casework intervention, while other programs have been predicated on views that link delinquency to deficiencies in the social order, such as lack of meaningful educational or work roles for youngsters. These discordant views of "the delinquency problem" have produced a heterogeneous mixture of diversion program strategies.

The Portland State University consultants provided a good deal of information and assistance to the Office of Juvenile Justice in the resolution of planning issues and questions. The university group (1) prepared a review of the theoretical and research literature on diversion, which ultimately became incorporated into the federal program announcement; [31] (2) developed a detailed program model outlining the central features of a diversion strategy focused on youth development activities, the provision of meaningful social roles to youngsters, and kindred related efforts; [32] and (3) devised an evaluation plan to accompany the program model.[33] Significant elements of the program model were incorporated into the final guidelines issued by the Office of Juvenile Justice in the program announcement, which

---

[31] Michael DeShane, Gerald F. Blake, and Don C. Gibbons, "Juvenile Diversion: Issues and Strategy," and "Appendix" (Portland, Ore.: Portland State University, 1975), mimeographed.

[32] James Galvin, Gerald F. Blake, and Don C. Gibbons, "Model Program: Youth Diversion Project" (Portland, Ore.: Portland State University, 1975), mimeographed.

[33] James Galvin, Gerald F. Blake, and Don C. Gibbons, "Evaluation Plan: LEAA Discretionary Funding Program for Youth Diversion" (Portland, Ore.: Portland State University, 1975), mimeographed.

was issued in April 1976.[34] This program announcement specifies that funding requests will be entertained only from organizations that develop diversion programs that are congruent with the program strategies outlined in the announcement. Additionally, applicants are required to conform to other federal guidelines which require that the diversion programs be subjected to detailed evaluation. Although our account here is quite brief, one can see in this experience some indications of a theoretically informed comprehensive planning process. Finally, we would argue that maximum benefit from public funds is most likely to be produced by other planning efforts along these lines.

SUMMARY

This chapter has sketched some of the major developments occurring since 1965 in the crime-fighting initiative and the federal funding program for crime control in the United States. This chapter also described the growth of criminal justice planning and the inadequacies of that activity to date.

Federally funded attacks upon the crime problems of modern society grew out of the 1967 report of the President's Commission on Law Enforcement and Administration of Justice.[35] We noted that the commission report placed heaviest emphasis upon *ameliorative* efforts devoted to dealing with the "root causes" of crime and major improvements in the general quality of life in the United States, rather than upon law enforcement–oriented crime *control* measures. The ameliorative proposals of the commission report were not spelled out in detail, nor was a price tag identified for them, but it seems clear enough that massive social and economic reforms were implied in that report. Had the commission recommendations been followed, they would probably have required such large-scale steps as federally

---

[34] Law Enforcement Assistance Administration, *Program Announcement.* However, we would also note that the federal program guidelines were somewhat ambiguous and would allow a number of different diversion strategies to compete for funds. The consultants were not entirely successful in their efforts to persuade the Office of Juvenile Justice to opt for a single, detailed program model. The final program guidelines probably represent a compromise designed to satisfy a number of competing interests.

[35] President's Commission on Law Enforcement, *Challenge of Crime.*

directed efforts at major income redistribution, massive societal planning, and movement toward some form of state socialism. The commission recommendations, however, could not have been implemented
through the relatively paltry sums that have been allocated to LEAA.

But, as we have seen, the commission report was followed by
the Omnibus Crime Control and Safe Streets Act of 1968, rather than
by responses that were keyed to the commission recommendations.
Federal funds have been provided for a "war on crime" in which the
domestic criminal targets are principally persons engaged in street
crimes and other garden-variety offenses. Relatively little has been
done about consumer fraud, white-collar crime, organized crime, or
other lawbreaking by more powerful citizens. Then, too, the image
of criminals that has dominated in efforts to date is one that characterizes them as domestic aliens and enemies. Garden-variety offenders
have become domestic "gooks" in the "war on crime."

There are a number of explanations for the federal response
to the crime problem, which moved away from the commission recommendations and toward crime control endeavors, some of which have
already been discussed in this chapter. Doubtless one major influence
centers on the cancer of the Vietnam War, which forced the Congress
and the Johnson administration to abandon "Great Society" efforts so
that heroic sums of federal money could be diverted to the war.
Whatever the reasons for the direction taken by the federal government, only a modest sum of federal money has been devoted to the
fight against crime.

The federal crime-fighting effort has been subjected to frequent criticism over its lifetime, with much of the negative commentary centering on the failure of LEAA to encourage sustained,
sophisticated criminal justice planning. A large part of this chapter
has discussed the problems that have plagued efforts to move in the
direction of comprehensive criminal justice planning. Chapter 3
continues that discussion, with more specific attention to some of the
organizational problems that must be overcome if sound planning
is to become a key ingredient of the criminal justice machinery.

3

Organizational Impediments to Planning

INTRODUCTION

In recent years a number of theorists have offered conceptual frameworks for criminal justice planning in which the case has been made for characterizing the criminal and juvenile justice machinery as a system. These theorists have elaborated at some length upon a basic point: Those things that are done about crime and to offenders in American society are influenced, at least in part, by public sentiment and public preferences concerning crime control. These same commentators have argued that the component parts of the criminal justice apparatus ought to function together as an integrated or coordinated system, although nearly all would agree that they fail to do so adequately at present. We shall examine some of these analytical conceptualizations of the system elements of criminal justice in detail in Chapter 4. The present chapter centers principally on a description of the current structure of the criminal justice enterprise and the impediments that this structure creates for planning.

PUBLIC OPINION AND JUSTICE PLANNING

The police, judges, correctional administrators, and others who toil in the criminal justice vineyard can often be found verbalizing arguments for some correctional or criminal justice policy or another taking the form that "the public demands" the policy. So, too, it is with many legislators, who join their advocacy of some punitive measure or bit of correctional legislation with statements that the actions reflect the wishes of the public. But very little evidence is actually at hand on the question of citizens' opinions about the criminal justice system.[1] Doubtless it is true that legislators and administrators of criminal justice programs do often endeavor to attune their actions to what they perceive to be the preferences of the citizenry, but this process is shot through with guesswork by the policymaker concerning the views of the public.

One of the unequivocal conclusions to be drawn from the relatively meager body of empirical evidence regarding citizens' opinions and the criminal justice system is that a principle of "out of sight, out of mind" often operates. That is, a number of studies of public views regarding punishment, corrections, and kindred topics indicate that laymen frequently have only hazy ideas, at best, regarding the operations of the justice system. For example, in one investigation in San Francisco, Don Gibbons reported that citizens knew about a few flamboyant or bizarre cases of criminality but had almost no detailed or accurate knowledge of the workings of the law enforcement, judicial, or correctional systems.[2] Similar results turned up in a study commissioned by the state Assembly Committee on Criminal Pro-

---

[1] Many of the existing studies on this topic are reviewed in Don C. Gibbons and Joseph F. Jones, *The Study of Deviance* (Englewood Cliffs, N.J.: Prentice-Hall, 1975), pp. 68–70.

[2] Don C. Gibbons, "Who Knows What about Correction?" *Crime and Delinquency,* 9 (April 1963), 137–44.

cedure in California,[3] and in still another probing of these matters by the Joint Commission on Correctional Manpower and Training.[4]

Several investigations have been conducted in recent years regarding the penalties that laymen regard as appropriate for offenders of different kinds. These studies seem to indicate both that citizens' preferences regarding the handling of offenders are congruent with actual policies for the most part and also that some exceptions exist, in which laymen would penalize certain offenders more heavily or less harshly than does the justice system. For example, those observations flow out of a study by Rose and Prell,[5] another by Gibbons,[6] and an inquiry regarding the juvenile court by Howard Parker.[7]

However, one might wonder whether public views regarding punishment might not be hardening under the influence of various contemporary conservative spokesmen such as James Q. Wilson, who has been counseling the construction of more prisons and incapacitation of larger numbers of offenders.[8] A recent study by Clayton Hartjen and Daniel Carratura is instructive on this issue.[9] They found in a New Jersey survey that citizens answering a questionnaire opted generally for punishments for offenders that were harsher than

[3] Assembly Committee on Criminal Procedure, *Deterrent Effects of Criminal Sanctions* (Sacramento: California State Legislature, 1968).

[4] Joint Commission on Correctional Manpower and Training, *The Public Looks at Crime and Corrections* (Washington, D.C., 1968). Also see Michael J. Hindelang, *Public Opinion Regarding Crime, Criminal Justice and Related Topics* (Washington, D.C.: Law Enforcement Assistance Administration, 1975).

[5] Arnold M. Rose and Arthur E. Prell, "Does the Punishment Fit the Crime? A Study in Social Valuation," *American Journal of Sociology*, 61 (November 1955), 247–49.

[6] Don C. Gibbons, "Crime and Punishment: A Study in Social Attitudes," *Social Forces*, 45 (June 1969), 391–97.

[7] Howard Parker, "Juvenile Court Actions and Public Response," in Peter G. Garabedian and Don C. Gibbons, eds., *Becoming Delinquent* (Chicago: Aldine, 1970), pp. 252–65.

[8] James Q. Wilson, *Thinking about Crime* (New York: Basic Books, 1975). For a critical review of Wilson's proposals, see Jerome H. Skolnick, "Are More Jails the Answer?" *Dissent*, 23 (Winter 1976), 95–97. Also a series of reviews of Wilson's book by Werner J. Einstadter, Roy Lotz, Richard Moran, Richard Quinney, and Jackson Toby, *Contemporary Sociology*, 5 (July 1976), 410–18.

[9] Clayton A. Hartjen and Daniel Carratura, "Attitudes toward Crime and Punishment: A Comparative Analysis," *International Journal of Contemporary Sociology*, forthcoming.

the legally prescribed penalties and also more severe than the choices made by a group of probation officers.

These studies are too limited for us to have much confidence in them as guides to the state of public opinion regarding criminal justice practices. Then, too, these inquiries have all followed a general methodology in which individual citizens have been given questionnaires that elicit their opinions. These studies tell us something about the views that emerge when we ask laymen for their opinions. At the same time, they tell us little or nothing about which of these anonymous individuals manage to make their voices heard by legislators and criminal justice administrators and by what means. In short, these investigations are not very revealing on the question of *which opinions have the greatest impact upon decision makers.*

It seems reasonable enough to conjecture that policymakers are most frequently bombarded by a cacophony of public views and interest group representations that urge them to move in many different directions. It makes relatively little sense to speak of public opinion on criminal justice in American society, implying that there is some general consensus among citizens on law enforcement, judicial, and correctional questions. Although data are lacking to demonstrate this assertion in detail, we suspect that legislators and administrators face a continuous situation of being besieged by discordant demands from various segments of the public. If that is the case, value conflict and the lack of a clear mandate from the public in whose name the criminal justice system is supposed to operate probably stand as the major impediments to system planning.

ORGANIZATIONAL IMPEDIMENTS

The Justice Nonsystem

Daniel Glaser, in his *Strategic Criminal Justice Planning*, has made the point that comprehensive planning cannot be done by a single component within the criminal justice machinery acting alone because of the interdependence of the system parts.[10] However, inter-

---

[10] Daniel Glaser, *Strategic Criminal Justice Planning* (Rockville, Md.: National Institute of Mental Health, 1975), p. 5.

dependent planning has not been characteristic of criminal justice agencies.

One of the major difficulties in implementing planning in the criminal justice system, whether it be short range or more comprehensive, is that historically, integrated activities of any kind between the component parts of the system have been little evident. We concede that some examples of cooperative or integrative efforts have existed between various criminal justice agencies, but these have usually centered on issues of the moment. One can cite, for example, the informal arrangements existing between juvenile courts and law enforcement agencies in many communities where written or unwritten policy agreements provide that certain youngsters will be diverted from the court intake process by the police if they have been involved in minor transgressions such as status offenses or petty misconduct. Operations of this kind have usually been initiated by juvenile court authorities as a way to reduce detention intake or to give a harried court probation staff and judge more time to devote to more serious offenders. A second example might be the close cooperation that has traditionally existed between prosecutors, judges, and adult probation and parole officers in devising interrelated operational procedures for the handling of adult offenders. But this intrasystem cooperation and planning has been operations focused and more a matter of convenience to one or another of the agencies than a deliberate effort at systems-oriented functioning.

The organizational conflicts and fractures that characterize the criminal justice apparatus and which frustrate efforts at integrative planning are numerous, complex, and often quite intractable, so that some extended commentary about them is in order. We ought not to suppose that the components of the criminal justice machinery will coalesce into a coherent, coordinated operation merely by our declaring them to constitute a system. To the extent that a justice system can be developed, it will have to come about through sustained efforts to deal with the conflicts that currently plague the law enforcement, judicial, and correctional processes.

It ought to be acknowledged at the outset that some of the interorganizational problems we will discuss are "fixed" or virtually incapable of being reduced markedly, while others are matters about which a good deal can be done. An example of the former would be the endemic quarrels between police agencies and correctional programs in which police officers complain bitterly about probation workers' putting offenders "back on the streets" almost immediately after they have been arrested. Police officers who are charged with "making the streets safe for citizens" are not likely to look favorably upon the decisions of correctional workers that stem from their mandate to treat and rehabilitate offenders. The policeman is not likely to be persuaded by the argument that, in the long run, correctional efforts will contribute as much to effective crime control as will enforcement policies, particularly given the paucity of evidence that demonstrates that correctional treatment is effective. In short, efforts to do away entirely with these conflicts beween the police and other criminal justice workers are probably doomed to failure. Even so, it may be that some attenuation of these quarrels between policemen and other justice system representatives might be brought about through training and educational programs within police departments and other justice network agencies, by higher employment standards, and by other efforts.

The other side of the coin is that some of the organizational problems that now characterize the criminal justice apparatus are amenable to efforts directed at reducing them. As one case in point, the employees of component organizations or agencies often disagree on such issues as the causes of crime and delinquency. Although it might be a rather difficult task to bring about increased consensus on questions of etiology, it is a manageable chore. There is a body of empirical evidence on crime and delinquency which can be examined and studied, and about which reasonable conclusions can be reached.

Conflicting Goals, Objectives, and Skills

Let us examine some of the organizational problems that impede efforts at justice system building and integrative planning. *First, each component of the criminal justice system, despite how one might attempt to bend the reality, has quite different primary goals and objectives.* Even though the criminal justice process is often represented as a rational continuum of activities on the part of involved agencies, there are clear-cut distinctions between the basic goals and objectives of these components. As these goals and objectives are translated into operational policies by each of the agencies, some degree of interagency tension is unavoidable. It is nearly inevitable that law enforcement administrators who stress detection and apprehension goals and who perceive themselves as being charged by the public with crime reduction will react negatively to liberalized plea bargaining or sentencing at the prosecutorial and court levels and, in like fashion, to a parole board agency policy of releasing large numbers of inmates. This conflict often shows up quite clearly in the vociferous complaints of individual police officers regarding "lenient judges" or "soft-headed probation officers." Conversely, correctional agents stressing rehabilitative aims are likely to respond with equal or greater acrimony to the law enforcement agency that "hassles" offenders on probation or parole and which in their view forces these individuals into new crimes.

These differences in goals and objectives among the criminal justice subsystems, as translated into operations policy, not only create tensions between agencies that must be dealt with continually through discussions and negotiations but also consume the time and energy of key personnel that might well be given over to more constructive and forward-looking planning relationships.[11]

Second, each of the subagencies of the criminal justice system emphasizes different skill orientations on the part of subagency managers and staffs. These variations complicate the planning task when individuals of varying professional orientations, value systems, and managerial perspectives attempt to think and act in terms of a "criminal justice system." Skill specialization differences contribute to the fractures in the criminal justice system because they place strong emphasis on individual agency concerns to the detriment of total system needs.

Divergent Policy Sources

A third obstacle to planning arises because the various subsystems of the criminal justice system march to different drummers, for they are subject to policy direction from a variety of political systems, ranging from federal to state, county, and city levels.[12] These political entities in turn respond to influences from various self-interest groups. For instance, the broad policy directives given the chief of police on

---

[11] For one valuable discussion of the techniques used by correctional administrators in dealing with the administrative problems facing them, see Elmer K. Nelson, Jr., and Catherine H. Lovell, *Developing Correctional Administrators* (Washington, D.C.: Joint Commission on Correctional Manpower and Training, 1969).

[12] This matter has been discussed at some length by Blair G. Ewing, "Criminal Justice Planning: An Assessment," *Criminal Justice Review,* 1 (Spring 1976), 124–26. He notes that the criminal justice machinery is a system in which the system components are dominant and to a considerable degree independent of each other.

the city level are not necessarily compatible with the policies of an elected district attorney, nor are the interests of state corrections officials in expanding community-based residential programs for adult offenders likely to find favor with organized local groups that view such facilities as potential threats to life and property of citizens, as well as raising the specter of declining residential values. Obviously, serious planning efforts between criminal justice agencies would be most successful if similar policy commitments existed among the various policymaking and influence groups, but the fact is that the subcomponents of the criminal justice system are responsive in different ways to diverse political and organized groups. Such a situation impedes interagency planning and makes truly innovative planning an even more remote possibility.

To this point, our discussion has drawn attention to a number of internal variations among component agencies within the criminal justice field which make cooperative activities and planning difficult. We do not have any magical cure for this situation. However, some mention ought to be made of recent steps toward the creation of criminal justice "superagencies" in several states, which have been undertaken in part in order to increase interagency coordination. Daniel Skoler has reported a survey of six states that have recently grouped together two or more criminal justice component agencies into a "superagency." [13] Although the specific superagency plans differ between Kentucky, Maryland, Montana, North Carolina, New Jersey, and Pennsylvania, in each of these states, police, correctional, and/or judicial operations have been merged into a single organizational entity. Skoler reports that these superagencies have been relatively successful in mitigating some of the chronic organizational problems discussed in this chapter. He notes that "what distinguishes this group of States is the combination of at least two or more elements of State-level police, correctional, prosecution, and defense functions, demonstrating that separate components of the system can live, interact, and function under a common administrative umbrella, along with a miscellany of other criminal justice related functions." [14]

---

[13] Daniel L. Skoler, "Antidote for the Nonsystem? State Criminal Justice Superagencies," *State Government*, 49 (Winter 1976), 308; and Skoler, "Correctional Unification: Rhetoric, Reality, and Potential," *Federal Probation*, 40 (March 1976), 14–20.

[14] Skoler, "Antidote for the Nonsystem?" p. 4.

Short-Range Crises vs. Planning

A fourth organizational problem hindering system cooperation arises outside of individual agencies or components. Criminal justice agencies are buffeted about by demands of various influence groups that current issues and problems be addressed immediately to the neglect of long-range planning needs. Local political and organized groups, for example, that express concern over increased delinquency or crime rates to law enforcement agencies or the judiciary and which demand tougher measures to be directed at lawbreakers usually have little awareness of overcrowded juvenile and adult institutions at the state level. Responses by local criminal justice agencies that are intended to do something about the crime problem are likely to have system reverberations not anticipated by local groups. The state corrections agency that administers the juvenile and adult institutions in such a situation would find it difficult to initiate a planning effort that would mitigate its own problems of institutional overcrowding and simultaneously respond to local demands for dramatic actions. In short, since the separate criminal justice agency components will never be neatly synchronized, the need for intersystem planning becomes all the more important, and all the more difficult to achieve because of the disharmonies in the system itself.

Disagreement about Causation and Crime Control

A fifth factor contributing to the absence of integrative planning in the criminal justice field is the confusion and disagreements that exist over causes, treatment, management, and prevention of crime and delinquency. Each segment of the justice system has particular and different perspectives on delinquent and criminal behavior.[15] Law en-

---

[15] Of course, individuals within these agencies also vary in their perceptions of offenders and criminality. Even so, police officers as a group are more likely to view criminals in a more hostile manner than are probation officers or other correctional workers. For one useful discussion of this matter of divergent perspectives, see Nicholas A. Reuterman and Desmond S. Cartwright, "Practitioner's Views of Delinquency Causation: A Consideration in Comprehensive Criminal Justice Planning," *Criminal Justice and Behavior*, 3 (March 1976), 67–84.

forcement officers may see delinquents or criminals as "bad apples" and pay little attention to sociological views of causation. Probation or parole officers often see the lawbreaker as an unfortunate product of family and neighborhood influences, whereas law enforcement officers view the offender as someone who should be locked up for the protection of the community. Probation or parole officers believe that the deviant individual has the potential to respond to one or more treatment approaches, either under supervision or in a community-based program. This dichotomy of perspective and response toward criminality is as old as society itself.

This conflict over the causes of deviance and regarding appropriate control strategies is a complex matter. In part, the disagreements that are commonplace among criminal justice employees revolve around questions of fact having to do with the etiology of lawbreaking or the efficacy of some intervention strategy. As one illustration, we offer the case of psychological hypotheses about delinquency. As we shall see in Chapter 5, many supporters can be found for the *interpersonal maturity levels theory,* which contends that delinquents are less interpersonally competent than are nondelinquents.[16] Our own reading of the existing empirical evidence regarding psychological problems among offenders leads us to the conclusion that the interpersonal maturity levels theory is invalid.[17] Moreover, it does not seem unreasonable to assume that others would draw the same conclusion upon examining the available data. In short, this specific quarrel revolves around questions of fact and ought to be amenable to resolution through factual evidence. The same point can be made regarding quarrels about such questions as whether group counseling is an effective correctional stratagem.[18] There is a relatively abundant supply of hard evidence that points unequivocally to the conclusion that it is not efficacious.

We acknowledge that factual quarrels do not always dissipate completely in the face of empirical evidence. The criminological literature is full of continuing disagreements regarding the precise extent to which some factor or another is implicated in lawbreaking. Many of

---

[16] Ted Palmer, "The Youth Authority's Community Treatment Project," *Federal Probation,* 38 (March 1974), 3–14.

[17] Don C. Gibbons, "Differential Treatment of Delinquents and Interpersonal Maturity Levels Theory: A Critique," *Social Service Review,* 44 (March 1970), 22–33.

[18] Gene Kassebaum, David A. Ward, and Daniel Wilner, *Prison Treatment and Parole Survival* (New York: John Wiley, 1971).

the research findings at hand are equivocal, being limited in one way or another, such that moderate disagreements about the facts are commonplace even on matters that are factual issues.

Ideological Conflict

Many of the seemingly factual issues that divide criminal justice workers, legislators, citizens, and other individuals, however, turn out not to be factual questions at all. Rather, many of the quarrels regarding the nature of deviance or appropriate ways of responding to it are, at heart, indicators of fundamental value positions. For example, when a police officer characterizes a Skid Road denizen as a "crummy wino" at the same time that a social worker calls for a medical approach to the "sick alcoholic," we are faced with conflicting perspectives that have relatively little to do with the hard facts concerning the nature of chronic alcoholism. Similarly, arguments between those who call for repressive police measures to be directed at "garden-variety" offenders and who are unconcerned about white-collar crime, on the one hand, and those who call instead for more attention to shoddy workmanship in the Alaska pipeline project, political corruption, or large-scale business crime, have relatively little to do with questions of fact.

The thrust of these remarks is that characterological contentions that offenders are "psychopaths," "weak," "sick," and so forth, often masquerade as statements of fact but are more properly to be seen as value-laden judgments that reflect various ideological postures taken by individuals. For example, there is little objective empirical evidence to show that chronic alcoholism is an illness parallel in form to influenza, measles, or diabetes. Instead, those who urge us to look at Skid Road alcoholics as "sick" persons are moved to do so basically out of feelings that urban derelicts have had little to do with determining their fate, hence they should not be subjected to punitive action. Conversely, the claim that the Skid Roader is "socially inadequate" reveals a different ideological posture regarding individual responsibility for deviant acts.

The same point holds for many policy recommendations for the control of crime. Proposals for mandatory jail terms for certain types of offenders, longer prison sentences, and the like, rarely arise out of empirical evidence showing that jail terms or lengthier prison sentences (or more lenient measures, for that matter) have any noticeable impact upon the crime problem. Similarly, those who recommend the restoration of capital punishment are influenced more by retributive sentiments than they are by hard evidence showing that the death penalty is an effective deterrent measure. These recommendations reveal moral or ideological positions which hold that certain lawbreakers "deserve" lesser or greater punishment.

Discordant value sets or ideological orientations among criminal justice administrators, planners, policy or advisory board members, interest groups, and citizens represent major obstacles to comprehensive planning. As Bolan has commented: "This is crucial terrain for planners, since values permeate all aspects of planning." [19]

The value and ideological issue is pervasive in all public policy formation and decision making. But it is particularly critical in the criminal justice field because of the nature of that clientele and the multiplicity of opinions on causation and appropriate responses to the crime and delinquency problem, to say nothing of the political volatility of the problem. Thus the criminal justice process can be said to be particularly vulnerable to value polarizations that occur both at the program and at the planning levels. Walter B. Miller has discussed the question of ideology and criminal justice policy at length. He argues that

> ideology and its consequences exert a powerful influence on the policies and procedures of those who conduct the enterprise of criminal justice, and the degree and kinds of influence go largely unrecognized. Ideology is the permanent hidden agenda of criminal justice.[20]

What is the nature of ideology? Let us borrow Miller's characterization:

> The term "ideology" may be used in many ways. It will be used here only to refer to a set of general and abstract beliefs or assumptions about the correct or proper state of things, particularly with respect to the moral order and political arrangements, which serve

---

[19] Richard S. Bolan, "Mapping the Planning Terrain," in David R. Godschalk, ed., *Planning in America: Learning From Turbulence* (Washington, D.C.: American Institute of Planners, 1974), p. 22.

[20] Walter B. Miller, "Ideology and Criminal Justice Policy: Some Current Issues," *Journal of Criminal Law and Criminology*, 64 (June 1973), 142.

to shape one's positions on specific issues. Several aspects of ideology as used in this sense should be noted. First, ideological assumptions are generally preconscious rather than explicit, and serve, under most circumstances, as unexamined presumptions underlying positions taken openly. Second, ideological assumptions bear a strong emotional charge. This charge is not always evident, but it can readily be activated by appropriate stimuli, in particular by direct challenge. During the process of formation, ideological premises for particular individuals are influenced by a variety of informational inputs, but once established they become relatively impervious to change, since they serve to receive or reject new evidence in terms of a self-contained and self-reinforced system.[21]

At various points in his analysis of value conflicts, Miller makes the case that criminal justice policies are most frequently determined on the basis of these ideological positions, rather than on a foundation of hard evidence. According to Miller:

The range of issues, problems, areas of endeavor, and arenas of activity relevant to the criminal justice enterprise is enormous. Given the vastness of the field relative to the availability of resources, decisions must be made as to task priorities and resource allocation. Ideology plays a paramount but largely unrecognized role in this process, to the detriment of other ways of determining priorities. Ideologized selectivity exerts a constant influence in determining which problem areas are granted greatest significance, which projects are supported, what kinds of information are gathered and how research results are analyzed and interpreted. Divergent resource allocation policies of major federal agencies can be viewed as directly related to the dominant ideological orientation of the agency.[22]

Miller discusses the philosophical underpinnings of the ideological positions of those engaged in the criminal justice field on issues ranging from the nature of crime to opinions on the appropriate operational focus of criminal justice agencies. Applied to the planning forum, Miller's typology would place those engaged in criminal justice

---

21 Ibid., p. 142.

22 Ibid., p. 152.

planning in a series of pigeonholes on the left and right of a centrist position on these issues:

> For the right, the paramount value is order—and ordered society based on a pervasive and binding morality—and the paramount danger is disorder—social, moral, and political. For the left, the paramount value is justice—a just society based on a fair and equitable distribution of power, wealth, prestige, and privilege—and the paramount evil is injustice—the concentration of valued social resources in the hands of a privileged minority.[23]

Miller sums up this disagreement as revolving around two value-laden positions: whether "order with justice" or "justice with order" should be the guiding principle of the criminal justice enterprise. The central task for criminal justice action and planning, according to Miller, is to work to reduce ideological intensification, bring the hidden ideological agenda of the criminal justice enterprise out into the open, and to make possible the opportunity to release the energy now consumed in partisan conflict for a more direct and effective engagement of the problems of crime control or reduction.

Miller concedes that his prescription for resolution of polarization is overly optimistic and overly simple. He speculates that at this present time in the history of the United States, major kinds of social adaptation can occur only through turbulent ideological social movements—and the costs of such processes must be borne in order to achieve the benefits they will ultimately confer. As a result, he suggests that ideological intensification, with all its dangers and drawbacks, may be a necessary component of effective social adaptation, and the ideologist must be seen as playing a necessary role in the process of social change.

However, in the context of his discussion, Miller also offers a view that is allied with that of traditional planning practitioners by suggesting that the detrimental effects of ideological intensification may potentially be blunted (to avoid the extremes of distortion, rigidity, and intolerance) by (1) clarifying when possible the distinction between "fact" and "value," and (2) granting a degree of validity to a counterview in order to arrive at compromise. Thus, while he describes in detail the range of polarization, the working or learning

---

[23] Ibid., p. 148.

arena (that is, the "predominant" views on a given issue) actually may be much more contracted and subject to compromise.

Ideological conflict is one of the primary reasons for the lack of interagency planning efforts, since it involves fundamental value issues which have both individual and organizational salience. Although frequent compromises have been reached among criminal justice agencies regarding these value issues, these have been on a "modus vivendi" level and do not represent lasting conflict resolution arrived at through discussion and planning Diversity of opinion on causes, prevention, treatment, and management of crime and delinquency will continue to exist, so that it is unlikely that polarization will simply disappear once it has been identified. But, we suggest that value issues must be dealt with openly by criminal justice agencies so that operational compromises extend beyond an expediency and opportunism that is detrimental to the criminal justice planning process and ultimately to justice system cohesiveness.

Lack of Baseline Data for Planning

A sixth factor limiting criminal justice system comprehensive planning efforts is the lack of uniform data systems both for management information and for research purposes. The inadequacy of information systems in the administration of criminal justice agencies has been noted repeatedly since the publication of the report of the President's Commission on Law Enforcement and Administration of Justice [24] and the statement of the National Advisory Commission on Criminal Justice Standards and Goals.[25] Data systems have usually been operations oriented, designed for specific budgetary and management needs of the individual agencies, although more recently LEAA emphasis and funds have been directed toward the development of state and local integrated criminal information systems. But, to date, there has been little interdependence among statistical information systems.

Similarly, on the research front, many research questions have been thwarted at the asking stage because of the lack of adequate

---

[24] The President's Commission on Law Enforcement and Administration of Justice, *The Challenge of Crime in a Free Society* (Washington, D.C.: Government Printing Office, 1967).

[25] National Advisory Committee on Criminal Justice Standards and Goals, *A National Strategy to Reduce Crime* (Washington, D.C., 1973).

data.[26] To be sure, criminal justice administrators have sometimes been chary of research because of its demands on agency time and energy, as well as being apprehensive about possible research outcomes, but this research reluctance has also been a reflection of the inadequacy of data systems. Research-generated baseline data are crucial in planning; hence this lack of adequate uniform, relevant, and reliable information sabotages planning efforts at the outset.

Additional factors are undoubtedly behind the dearth of cooperative planning in the criminal justice field. Our cursory analysis emphasizes that criminal justice is to a large extent an uneasy mix of agencies with separate missions and with sometimes converging and even overlapping functions rather than a coherent system attuned to the necessity of strategic planning.

ORGANIZATIONAL FRACTURES AND PLANNING STRATEGIES

We have presented a discouraging litany of obstacles and impediments to criminal justice planning, many of which involve ideological conflict and polarization. How are we to deal with these problems of heroic proportions, if at all? We have already taken note of Miller's recommendation that ideological positions be brought out into the open so that they might be discussed and perhaps reconciled, at least to some extent. Unfortunately, Miller's suggestions for the reduction of ideological polarization are not very detailed or specific.

John Friedmann has devoted considerable attention in his *Retracking America* to the central problem identified by Miller—the difficulty of formulating public policy in a pluralistic society characterized by discordant value preferences.[27] We shall take up Friedmann's commentary on planning in more detail in Chapter 6. One of the essentials of his argument is that we need to work toward the develop-

---

[26] However, Ewing has pointed out that there has virtually been a "data explosion" in recent years, so that the justice planner or administrator is now often faced with a somewhat different problem—how to manage and process the available information. Ewing, "Criminal Justice Planning."

[27] John Friedmann, *Retracking America* (New York: Anchor Books/Doubleday, 1973). Also see Donald N. Michael, *On Learning to Plan—And Planning to Learn* (San Francisco: Jossey-Bass, 1973).

ment of a "learning society," in which 25 million or more citizen participants would engage in a planning dialogue and process which he terms "transactive planning." These citizen-planners would work in planning groups of various sizes, studying the "societal guidance system(s)" that are responsible for problems in need of solution and developing plans for altering the guidance mechanisms. Societal guidance systems are those features of social structure that produce such phenomena as collective violence, criminality, mental illness, and so forth, as well as socially valued outcomes.

Real progress could probably be achieved toward planning goals if we were successful in restructuring society along the participatory lines suggested by Friedmann. But, as he acknowledges, his proposals are utopian and relatively vague, so that he does not provide much in the way of direction as to how the learning society might be achieved.[28]

Moving to some more concrete comments, Ewing has provided considerable insight into the difficulties associated with operating the criminal justice apparatus as a system.[29] Although there are significant managerial and operational differences among criminal justice agencies, he stresses the need for coordination and comprehensive planning, particularly in light of the amendments to the Crime Control Act of 1973, which require that state comprehensive plans contain a total, integrated analysis of the justice system which takes account of all aspects of the criminal justice operation.

This discussion of impediments to integrated systemwide planning in the criminal justice field leads to the question of what particular planning strategies are most viable for justice agencies, a matter about which Ewing is most vocal. As he indicates, LEAA has been supporting "comprehensive" planning and the articulation of overall statewide justice system plans. The "master plan" notion is also central to activities undertaken by the National Clearinghouse on Criminal Justice and Architecture, that is, the clearinghouse has been assisting states to develop long-range "master plans" for their entire criminal justice machinery.

Support for "comprehensive planning" or "master planning" in criminal justice is frequently voiced, and relatively few have argued

---

[28] We would also point out that Friedmann offers relatively little in the way of detailed description and analysis of the nature of the specific societal guidance systems that are involved in various collective phenomena.

[29] Ewing, "Criminal Justice Planning."

against these approaches. But perhaps master planning is an unwise and unproductive strategy, due to the organizational fissures and value conflicts noted in this chapter. Perhaps a more modest approach to justice planning has much to recommend it. The harsh reality of justice system conflicts may mean that the goal of developing broad, comprehensive master plans for entire state systems is largely unachievable or even completely unrealistic, given justice system realities. We need to examine the rationale for master planning and alternative strategies.

These discordant opinions about planning approaches in criminal justice are related to a vigorous dialogue that has been carried on by planning theorists for many years.[30] Many persons are pessimistic about the prospects for comprehensive social planning. For instance, Banfield considers effective planning to be an illusory goal because of (1) our inability to predict the future beyond a few years; (2) our inability to discover goals on which all can agree; (3) the decentralized character of the political system; and (4) the lack of knowledge of effective means to achieve ends.[31] Along the same line, Friedmann asserts that comprehensive planning is incompatible with the narrow interests involved in the competition for power and influence characteristic of any political system.[32] Braybrooke and Lindblom also point to deficiencies in the knowledge necessary for problem solving in the planning arena, including the absence of comprehensive information, the costliness of complex analyses, and the diverse forms that policy problems take.[33] Indeed, Lindblom is sufficiently disenchanted with the prospects for planning that he has opted for a minimum of it, in favor of "disjointed incrementalism." Disjointed incrementalism is his term for social processes involving disjointed and incremental

---

[30] Richard S. Bolan, "Emerging Views of Planning," *Journal of the American Institute of Planners*, 33 (July 1967), 233–45. Also see John Friedmann and Barclay Hudson, "Knowledge and Action: A Guide to Planning Theory," *Journal of the American Institute of Planners*, 40 (January 1974), 2–16.

[31] Edward C. Banfield, "The Use and Limitations of Metropolitan Planning in Massachusetts" (Paper presented at the Fifth Working Conference on Metropolitan Planning and Regional Development, Joint Center for Urban Studies, Metropolitan Area Planning Council, June 1965), pp. 12–14. See also Banfield, "Ends and Means in Planning," *UNESCO International Social Science Journal*, 11 (1959), 365–68.

[32] John Friedmann, "Introduction: The Study and Practice of Planning," *UNESCO International Social Science Journal*, 11 (1959), 336. However, he does not counsel us to abandon the planning goal. See Friedmann, *Retracking America*.

[33] David Braybrooke and Charles Lindblom, *A Strategy of Decision* (New York: Free Press, 1963), Chaps. 2 and 3.

problem-solving actions that grow out of economic circumstances, other social factors, and the pull and tug of competing interest groups.[34] According to this view, these processes will ensure that whatever social issue is missed by one disjointed and incremental action will be attended to by another; hence comprehensive planning is both unworkable and unnecessary.

Ewing indicates that over the years, justice planners have debated the advantages and disadvantages of at least three major planning approaches. The first of these, "master planning" (or blueprinting), involves the articulation of a complex plan to guide the future for a substantial period of time. Once this "grand design" is developed, relatively little attention is then given to implementation or revisions of the master plan. Ewing points out that this model has dominated in land-use planning but dismisses it as largely inapplicable to the criminal justice system. He does view master planning as possible within the correctional subsystem, because most states have a centralized adult and juvenile corrections agency, an identifiable client group, and specific program services (e.g., institutions, work release, probation and parole services). It may be possible to engage in comprehensive corrections planning where the only major disturbing influence external to the correctional component is fluctuations in numbers of sentenced or committed offenders entering the system. However, many correctional authorities would probably voice pessimism about master planning under the current condition of great system strain due to the jump in commitments and the trend toward "flat" sentences, both phenomena unexpected until recently and subjecting the corrections system to serious planning and program crises.

The second approach identified by Ewing, the research model, involves postponement of the development of plans until a detailed knowledge base is developed. Although an extensive body of research findings would be extremely useful and might help planners to resolve conflict issues, the problems of the justice system are often too pressing to allow us to wait for research findings before formulating action plans. Parenthetically, the impulse toward immediate action arising from the financial carrot-on-the-stick offered by LEAA has relegated research-based planning in criminal justice to a secondary role at the same time that huge sums have been spent on the continuation of traditional and ineffectual programs.

The third approach identified by Ewing, and the one he con-

[34] Charles Lindblom, *The Intelligence of Democracy: Decision-Making through Mutual Adjustment* (New York: Free Press, 1965).

siders the most appropriate for the criminal justice system, is the "incrementalist" or "process" approach. Incremental planning in criminal justice would involve independent planning and implementation activities being conducted on a continuing and relatively modest basis by justice system components, out of which it would be hoped that system improvement and efficiency would eventually result. Total planning for the entire system, particularly master plans projected a decade or so into the future, would receive much less attention. As noted earlier, incremental planning involves a planning process designed to produce successively better approximations of rational plans over time:

> The plans produced using this model are acknowledged to be incomplete, although they are also designed to improve steadily through a continuous process which involves feedback to the planner on the results of plan implementation, and then a better plan next time.[35]

The limitations of the incrementalist or process approach are acknowledged by Ewing, but because of the fractured nature of the criminal justice system, he sees no viable alternative to it. His recommendation is that we continue to emphasize systemwide planning and the coordination of the components of the criminal justice system within an incrementalist framework, largely within the structure of state planning agencies. He seems convinced that an incrementalist planning process will eventually result in improved criminal justice system planning.

The planning process that has evolved to date from the LEAA-funded programs is more similar to "disjointed incrementalism" than it is to Ewing's "rational incrementalism." Ewing has identified a model or approach that *should* be developing in criminal justice planning, but the actual history of planning since the inception of LEAA shows more the flavor of disjointed incrementalism.

We are in general agreement with Ewing's argument for incremental planning, as contrasted to undue stress upon master plans and grand designs, on the one hand, or a policy of "more research," on the other. There is urgency to the crime problem, so that we need to develop plans for attacking it. However, we also need to be on guard against papering over the real obstacles to planning and the short-

---

[35] Ewing, "Criminal Justice Planning," p. 130.

comings of current planning efforts. In particular, we ought not to disguise these obstacles and shortcomings by labeling them "rational incrementalism." We have some distance to go in justice planning before rational incrementalism becomes a reality. Ultimately, LEAA and state and regional planning agencies themselves will determine whether an observable shift occurs from a disjointed to a more rational incremental planning process.

SUMMARY

This chapter has enumerated many of the extraordinarily complex and difficult obstacles that have plagued efforts to bring about increased coordination of the activities of component agencies within the criminal justice apparatus. These organizational difficulties promise to continue to frustrate planning efforts. Indeed, some of the organizational fractures and conflicts considered here seem so intractable that one is tempted to throw up one's hands in despair and to abandon the planning goal.

But we do not suggest that the planning efforts be abandoned. Rather, sustained attention needs to be given to the creation of a more positive planning climate. We do not have any novel or dramatic solutions to the organizational problems of criminal justice to offer, beyond the proposals of Miller, Ewing, and others, centered on open communication, sustained dialogue, and efforts to identify and reduce value conflicts. It must be clear enough from our remarks in this chapter that we regard these obstacles to planning as matters that do not lend themselves to simple solutions. However, we shall return to the topic of conflict reduction in Chapter 7 where we will consider a number of more specific techniques for improving planning processes and diffusion of interorganizational disagreements.

4

Some Perspectives on Planning

INTRODUCTION

In this chapter we begin to move away from descriptive comments on the state of criminal justice planning toward some more conceptual and analytical observations about justice planning. Chapter 4 takes up a review of the literature, summarizing a number of relatively general perspectives on justice planning that have recently appeared.[1] Some

---

[1] At least one text on criminal justice planning has already appeared, but it focuses on short-range planning and emphasizes specific techniques and procedures to be applied to projects and problems. It has little to say about planning theory or the application of criminological knowledge to planning. See Michael E. O'Neill, Ronald F. Bykowski, and Robert S. Blair, *Criminal Justice Planning* (San Jose, Calif.: Justice Systems Development, 1976). The O'Neill, Bykowski, and Blair book is a useful complementary work to our text.

important contributions have been made to the emerging planning literature. Accordingly, we ought to begin an analysis of planning knowledge and technology by examining the existing literature, selecting those works of others on which we might build. We shall see from this review that much of what has appeared to this point has consisted of a mixture of general commentary about the need for planning, along with some brief discussion of planning concepts that may have some utility in planning. We hope to build upon these statements of others in Chapters 5, 6, and 7, by developing a more detailed and comprehensive planning framework than has appeared to date.

SOME VIEWS ON CRIMINAL JUSTICE PLANNING

The Criminal Justice Machinery as a System

We have already observed that several analysts have offered statements that stress the importance of conceptualizing the criminal justice apparatus as a system of interrelated parts made up of the police, courts, institutions, and other components.[2] These persons argue that only by looking at criminal justice agencies as parts of a coherent system can comprehensive planning succeed, for changes in one portion of the overall structure have ramifications for other segments of the system which must be anticipated when introducing innovations. Some sense of the criminal justice network can be derived from Figure 5, which illustrates the various component parts and decision points in the criminal machinery.

One such statement has been offered by Jim Munro, in which he contends that our efforts to understand the workings of justice system organizations will be severely handicapped if we approach them from a "closed system" approach that focuses only on the internal workings of the specific agency.[3] Instead, according to Munro, the

---

[2] For a general statement on social system "models" and system thinking in planning, along with comments on the implications of a systems framework for planning, see Robert R. Mayer, "Social System Models for Planners," *Journal of the American Institute of Planners,* 38 (May 1972), 130–39.

[3] Jim L. Munro, "Towards a Theory of Criminal Justice Administration: A General Systems Perspective," *Public Administration Review,* 31 (November–December 1971), 621–31; also see R. Gordon Cassidy, "A Systems Approach to Planning and Evaluation in Criminal Justice Systems," *Socio-Economic Planning Sciences,* 9 (December 1975), 301–12.

parts of the justice system should be examined in the light of an "open systems theory," which locates each component within an encompassing environment made up of other justice agencies and other influences. This discussion by Munro involves considerable use of such terms as "inputs," "throughputs," and "outputs," along with a number of diagrams that are intended to convey the nature of criminal justice systems. However, his analysis contains relatively little in the way of substantive details regarding the actual operation of the justice machinery and its components. Additionally, he has little to say about criminal justice planning activities, other than to make the implicit point that planners need to take account of the interrelationships of specific justice agencies. Munro's explication also demonstrates that the current criminal justice structure usually operates more as a nonsystem than it does as a finely tuned machine, in that many of the components of the overall apparatus tend to work at cross-purposes.

While the Munro article is fairly general, it does make the point that the criminal justice system has been characterized by a "closed system mentality," as reflected in the attitudes and actions of those who run the justice enterprise and those who provide the funding and ultimate policy direction, that is, the legislators and local elected officials. In this respect Munro correctly identifies and supplies a diagnosis for those difficulties encountered in criminal justice planning and decision making that are the basis of the many attacks directed toward the criminal justice system by both its sympathetic and its not so sympathetic critics.

Frederick Howlett and Hunter Hurst have presented a more detailed discussion of the system features of the criminal justice apparatus.[4] Their commentary is in the form of a taxonomic exercise which sets out a number of elements or dimensions that comprise the criminal justice system. Thus they remind us that criminal justice operates within a legal framework that identifies the forms of conduct that come under its purview. The system also must contend with patterns and amounts of crime that are determined by influences outside of itself, and it must take into account a variety of community expectations and forces that impinge upon it. Howlett and Hurst also list the process elements of the system, including law enforcement, prosecutors and defense attorneys, courts, probation and aftercare, institutions, and supportive services. Additionally, they note that in order to understand the workings of the system or to introduce

---

[4] Frederick W. Howlett and Hunter Hurst, "A Systems Approach to Comprehensive Criminal Justice Planning," *Crime and Delinquency*, 17 (October 1971), 345–54.

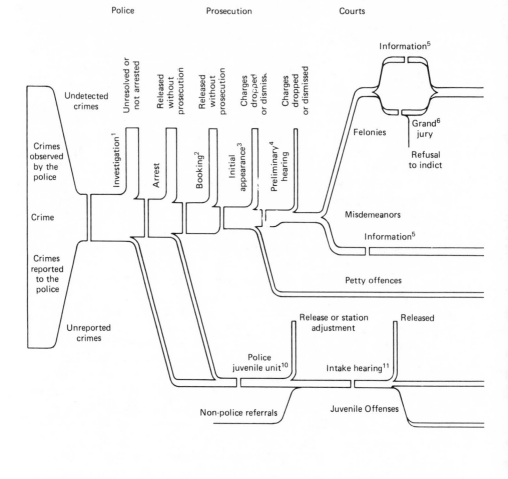

Police   Prosecution   Courts

Information[5]

Undetected crimes

Unresolved or not arrested

Released without prosecution

Released without prosecution

Charges dropped or dismiss.

Charges dropped or dismissed

Crimes observed by the police

Investigation[1]

Arrest

Booking[2]

Initial appearance[3]

Preliminary[4] hearing

Felonies

Grand[6] jury

Refusal to indict

Crime

Misdemeanors

Information[5]

Crimes reported to the police

Petty offences

Unreported crimes

Release or station adjustment

Released

Police juvenile unit[10]

Intake hearing[11]

Non-police referrals

Juvenile Offenses

1 May continue until trial.

2 Administrative record of arrest first stage at which temporary release on bail may be available.

3 Before magistrate, commissioner, or justice of peace, formal notice of charge, advice of rights, Budget Summary trials for party offenses usually conducted here without further processing.

4 Preliminary testing of evidence against defendent. Charge may be reduced. No separate pre-liminary hearing for misdemeanors in some systems.

5 Charge filed by prosecutor on basis of information submitted by police or citizens. Alternative to grand jury indictment often used in felonies, almost always in misdemeanors.

6 Reviews whether government evidence sufficient to justify trial. Some states have no grand jury system, others seldom use it.

FIGURE 5. A General View of the Criminal Justice System. This chart presents a simple yet comprehensive view of the movement of cases through the criminal justice system. Procedures in individual jurisdictions may vary from the pattern shown here. The differing weights of line, indicating the relative volumes of cases disposed of at various points in the system, is only suggestive because no nationwide data of this sort exist.

Corrections

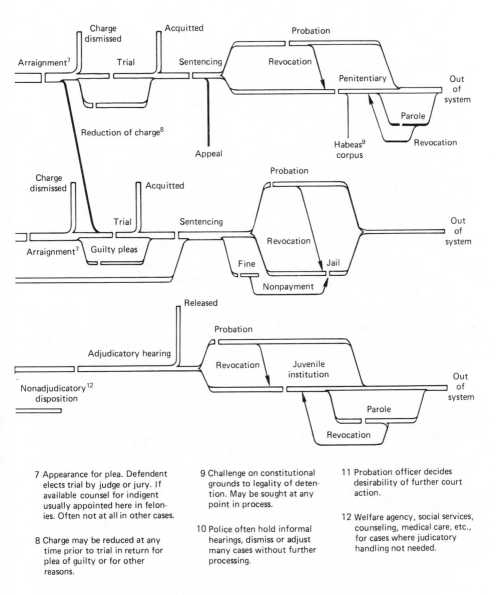

This chart is taken from the President's Commission on Law Enforcement and Administration of Justice, *The Challenge of Crime in a Free Society* (Washington, D.C.: Government Printing Office, 1967), pp. 8–9.

changes in it, the goals of the parts, the functional interrelations among those parts, the administrative policies of the specific agencies, and the information systems of the organizations must be identified. Finally, they indicate that the procedures and practices of agencies must be taken into account, along with their manpower resources, the nature of the clientele they process, their physical facilities, and the costs associated with the organization.

Howlett and Hurst's essay is similar to Munro's in that it contains a number of diagrams and a good deal of conceptual elaboration, but it is short on detailed probing of system activities. Howlett and Hurst make these points: (a) the activities of specific parts of the overall operation have consequences for other elements in the system, and (b) the contemporary justice machinery is surely not accurately described as an integrated system. Although this discussion is of value, its major contribution is the emphasis given to the study-consultation functions and process, in this case as carried out by the National Council on Crime and Delinquency, in reviewing criminal justice programs. While study and consultation are specific elements of the planning process, Howlett and Hurst frame them in the context of the NCCD approach, which is a mix of program change advocacy, political neutrality, and citizen action. Thus they conceptualize justice planning in the national study-consultation mode, which is helpful but does not deal directly with the techniques by which changes might be introduced at one point or another in the law enforcement, judicial, or correctional operations. In short, they present a mapping of the system from the perspective of the study-consultation functions but are relatively silent on the question of how that map might be altered, which is the central task of planning in the 1970s.

Some parallel comments can be made about still another of these expositions—a conceptual framework for planning by James Frank and Frederic Faust.[5] These authors begin by drawing attention to the lack of training and technical knowledge of planning principles characteristic of state and regional justice planners, so that their commentary revolves around an effort to apply urban and regional planning concepts to the development of a conceptual framework for these persons. In their discussion, they aver that policy planning involves ". . . the production of analytic information relative to the nature of the policy problem, alternative solutions, and likely impacts of policy and program adoptions." [6]

---

[5] James E. Frank and Frederic L. Faust, "A Conceptual Framework for Criminal Justice Planning," *Criminology*, 13 (August 1975), 271–96.

[6] Ibid., p. 273.

Not surprisingly, the conceptual dimensions identified by Frank and Faust parallel those noted by Howlett and Hurst. The former specify six key elements of the system-environment relationship, including the criminal law, crime patterns, system goals imposed by outside interests such as legislators and the general public, sanctions in the way of public endorsement of system programs, agency resources, and operating programs. Too, they make the relatively obvious point that when changes occur in one element, such as decriminalization that removes certain persons from system responsibility, the consequences of that development ramify to other parts of the system.

Frank and Faust also devote attention to identification of the policy-planning needs of the system. First, planners must be able to identify changes in the elements of the system-environment relationship, anticipate the effects of such changes on the system, and develop responses or adaptations to them. Second, policy planning requires skills in anticipating consequences of these responses or adaptations upon other parts of the system and in developing solutions to system disruptions brought about by changes introduced in some subsystem part. Third, policy planning calls for examination of alternative program stratagems and assessment of the financial and organizational costs that would accompany introduction of one or another of these program technologies.[7]

Frank and Faust also inform us that demands for planning are sometimes formalized ones, arising out of LEAA requirements and the like, while on other occasions, the demand for policy planning is relatively informal and inarticulate. They also enumerate the "key actors" in the "policy arena," which they list as the executive branch of state government, legislators, the judiciary, the client public, and nonclient publics such as the American Civil Liberties Union. Much of this commentary is useful in identifying some of the parameters within which planning takes place, but unfortunately this essay does not move much beyond some fairly self-evident observations.

These authors also present a "lexicon of policy analytic outputs," which is their way of referring to different kinds of planning

---

[7] This account of the planning process is parallel to Blumstein's characterization. See Alfred Blumstein, "A Model to Aid in Planning for the Total Criminal Justice System," in Leonard Oberlander, ed., *Quantitative Tools for Criminal Justice Planning* (Washington, D.C.: Law Enforcement Assistance Administration, 1975), p. 130. Blumstein enumerates the following steps in the planning process: (1) describe the current system; (2) project the future environment; (3) develop alternatives among which to chose; (4) analyze the impact of the alternatives ("pre-evaluation"); (5) allocate resources to the choices and implement them; (6) evaluate the impact ("post-evaluation"); (7) repeat the process on a regular and continuing basis.

products. This listing includes *policy problem structuring,* in which
efforts are directed at identification of the parameters of "the problem"
needing attention. An example of this type of output would be a
descriptive study of a cohort of prisoners processed through county
jails in order that the characteristics of these individuals might be
identified, including such things as age, sex, offense patterns, average
number of days held in jail before trial, and myriad other social
bookkeeping facts upon which plans for modifications in jail practices
might be constructed.

A second form of policy output is the *analysis of policy
alternatives,* in which the relative merits of several different programs
—such as probation and restitution, straight probation, or probation
combined with jail time—would be identified, in terms of associated
recidivism, program costs, and the like.

A third form of policy output consists of *program outcome
assessments,* which is a form of activity that others have identified as
program evaluation.[8] Although the dividing line between evaluation
of an *ongoing* program and the planning of change or adoption of
a new program is not a firm one, we would stress that criminal justice
planning involves more than simply the former. While a comprehensive evaluation of some existing program may be a highly useful
starting point for planned change, the evaluation itself probably
ought to be distinguished from planning efforts.

Policy analytic outputs also include *quantitative analysis of
service demand and delivery capacity,* which has to do with assessing
the effects of changes introduced into one part of the system upon
component segments of the total system. Finally, a *comprehensive
plan* is a policy output that "analyzes the entire criminal justice system
or substantial portion thereof and makes long-term recommendations
for operation of the system." [9] Frank and Faust offer some brief re-

---

[8] For some useful sources on program evaluation, see Daniel Glaser,
Routinizing Evaluation (Rockville, Md.: National Institute of Mental Health, 1975);
Stuart Adams, *Evaluative Research in Corrections* (Washington, D.C.: Law Enforce-
ment Assistance Administration, 1975); Florence Yospe, ed., *Program Evaluation in
Corrections: An Annotated Bibliography* (Portland: National Criminal Justice Educa-
tional Development Project, Portland State University, 1976); Don C. Gibbons, Barry
D. Lebowitz, and Gerald F. Blake, "Program Evaluation in Correction," *Crime and
Delinquency,* 22 (July 1976), 309–21; and Donald R. Weidman, John D. Waller,
Dona McNeil, Francine L. Tolson, and Joseph S. Wholey, *Intensive Evaluation for
Criminal Justice Planning Agencies* (Washington, D.C.: Law Enforcement Assistance
Administration, 1975).

[9] Frank and Faust, "Conceptual Framework," pp. 290–91.

marks regarding some of the major problems and obstacles to comprehensive planning, but they have little to say about the planning process itself. As a result, the summary judgment of their statement would be that while it is a useful enumeration of conceptual dimensions involved in planning, its principal utility is as a skeleton outline rather than a detailed substantive discussion of planning principles and technology.

Parenthetically, one other point that needs to be made about those endeavors to characterize the criminal justice machinery as a system is that not only is this structure a nonsystem in many ways but, additionally, it is sometimes better described as a criminal or juvenile *injustice* system. That is, the problems with the law enforcement and crime control apparatus often go deeper than lack of coordination among the components, for they frequently involve discriminatory processing of offenders. For example, there is considerable evidence pointing to sexist discrimination against females who are processed in courts or placed in training schools, racism in police enforcement activities, and other data pointing to inequitable and capricious actions taken against offenders.[10]

Another statement of a general planning model has been made by Nanus.[11] He emphasizes the institutionalization of a planning process within criminal justice agencies, including creation of a planning staff, planning task forces or committees, a planning cycle, and a planning information system. He presents a planning model in which five distinct planning tasks proceed in a continuous and systematic fashion. The types of planning are identified as

1. FUTURE STUDIES: involving development of forecasts of alternative futures on the basis of crime data, population and other demographic trends, changes in values and attitudes

---

[10] Much of the evidence on sexism in law enforcement and corrections is reviewed in Don C. Gibbons, *Delinquent Behavior*, 2nd ed. (Englewood Cliffs, N.J.: Prentice-Hall, 1976), pp. 169–89; and Gibbons, *Society, Crime and Criminal Careers*, 3rd ed. (Englewood Cliffs, N.J.: Prentice-Hall, 1977). Data on racial discrimination in law enforcement is reviewed in Gibbons, *Delinquent Behavior*, pp. 37–49; Gibbons, *Society, Crime, and Criminal Careers*, passim. A wealth of data on the inequities in the juvenile justice system is reported in Robert D. Vinter, Theodore M. Newcomb, and Rhea Kish, eds., *Time Out: A National Survey of Juvenile Correctional Programs* (Ann Arbor: National Assessment of Juvenile Corrections, University of Michigan, 1976).

[11] Burt Nanus, "A General Model for Criminal Justice Planning," *Journal of Criminal Justice*, 2 (Winter 1974), 345–56.

toward crime, legislation and court rulings, new technology, and a wide variety of other social, demographic, and economic variables;

2. POLICY PLANNING: defined as the establishment of broad objectives, definition of problems and opportunities, and development of policy guidelines;

3. STRATEGIC PLANNING: which is concerned with the identification and evaluation of program alternatives and the development of guidelines for tactical or operational planners;

4. OPERATIONAL PLANNING: which is short-term planning most likely reflected in cyclical budget planning;

5. IMPLEMENTATION, PLANNING, AND REVIEW: referring to the specific processes of implementation and assessment of plans.

The Nanus essay is most noteworthy for its emphasis on the need for planning mechanisms and for identifying functions engaged in by planning staffs. Like other statements reviewed to this point, it is relatively skimpy in terms of detailed comments on planning operations.

Strategic Criminal Justice Planning

One of the most comprehensive efforts to date to outline a number of dimensions and principles of criminal justice planning is found in Daniel Glaser's *Strategic Criminal Justice Planning*.[12] In that work, Glaser begins by differentiating *tactical* planning from *strategic* planning. Regarding the former, he notes that ". . . most long-established service agencies of government plan by projecting the past into the future. . . . Estimates of future needs are then made by extending these trends into the next 3, 5, or even 10 years. . . . Current practices and standards of service provide the primary basis

---

[12] Daniel Glaser, *Strategic Criminal Justice Planning* (Rockville, Md.: National Institute of Mental Health, 1975). Also see Glaser, *Adult Crime and Social Policy* (Englewood Cliffs, N.J.: Prentice-Hall, 1972), which is similar in content to his planning monograph. Additionally, see Gene Kassebaum, *Delinquency and Social Policy* (Englewood Cliffs, N.J.: Prentice-Hall, 1974). Although ostensibly dealing with social policy issues, this companion volume to Glaser's book is relatively silent on the issue of policies for delinquency control or reduction. Near the end of this book (p. 160), Kassebaum concludes: "It must be left to the reader to develop the policy implications of data on delinquent behavior and delinquency control programs."

for these estimates, although plans usually call for some upgrading of services, thus requiring additional funding." [13]

Glaser quite properly directs attention to the limitations of tactical planning, or what some others have termed *management control* or *allocative planning* and which Friedmann describes as concerned with the distribution of existing resources among competing users.[14] Glaser makes the case for strategic planning, involving innovative, comprehensive, long-range efforts to bring about structural changes in the criminal justice system. Strategic planning is a form of activity that he identifies as being comparable to Friedmann's "innovative planning." According to Glaser: "Therefore, strategic or innovative planning must be less inhibited than tactical or allocative planning in contemplating the alteration of long institutionalized organizational or even societal arrangements." [15]

Glaser devotes much attention to the identification of stages in the strategic planning process. He contends that, first, planners must initially gain an understanding of major social and economic trends and their likely future impact upon lawbreaking and social control responses to it. Second, they must identify the more specific causes of criminal behavior which are to be the target of intervention efforts. Third, they must devise policies for the allocation of resources and responsibilities among various agencies, both inside and outside the official justice system. These responsibilities have principally to do with identification of offender types, modification of their behavior, and preventive efforts. The fourth stage identified by Glaser consists of providing for steady improvement of planning in the future through the development of better baseline data on offender work loads, rigorous evaluation of intervention programs, and the like.[16] Glaser is clearly on the mark in this initial part of his monograph in his portrayal of the major ingredients of comprehensive and strategic criminal justice planning. He draws on Friedmann's position that the crime problem can only be addressed in terms of assessing and taking action to change the institutional arrangements that produce the phenomena.[17]

---

[13] Glaser, *Strategic Criminal Justice Planning*, p. 3.

[14] John Friedmann, *Retracking America* (New York: Anchor Books/Doubleday, 1973).

[15] Glaser, *Strategic Criminal Justice Planning*, p. 4.

[16] Ibid., pp. 7–9.

[17] Friedmann, *Retracking America*.

However, we are not so persuaded of the accuracy of Glaser's account of major societal trends now underway. For example, in another work he has conjectured that over the next two decades the offender population will come to include more whites and greater numbers of affluent citizens, due to welfare reforms and economic opportunity programs that will reduce poverty and economic precariousness.[18] Glaser also asserts that revolution is impossible in this country because the politically and economically powerful respond to the legitimate grievances of less advantaged citizens by orderly reforms:

> In countries such as the United States and Sweden for example, firmly institutionalized election procedures make the government frequently subject to peaceful change that reflects shifts in the public's political preferences. As the inclusion process accelerates, liberals win control of the government whenever there is much pressure for change, and long before radicals have enough support to gain power through either electoral or revolutionary methods. When liberals introduce reforms, the revolutionary movements lose support. Thus, whenever radicalism begins to gain support it is likely to accelerate reforms benefitting those to whom its potential appeal is greatest, but the reforms are enacted by liberal rather than radical governments.
>
> The foregoing discussion implies that revolution is impossible in the United States. Before any revolutionary cause obtains sufficient popular support to have any prospect of gaining power the policies that gave it support are championed effectively in the elected government, since competing candidates win or lose on the basis of their appeal to the populace. Thus any particular issue that the polls indicate much of the public endorses is also endorsed by many candidates and elected officials.[19]

There is considerable room for argument about the extent to which liberal reforms have occurred in the past in response to public agitation. Accordingly, a number of analysts would offer a less-sanguine view of the past than does Glaser. And, even if he is correct about

---

[18] Daniel Glaser, "Changes in Corrections during the Next 20 Years," in American Justice Institute, *Future of Criminal Justice Personnel: Position Papers* (Sacramento, Calif., 1972).

[19] Glaser, *Strategic Criminal Justice Planning*, pp. 22–23.

liberal reform being relatively prominent in the history of the country, he may well be considerably off the mark in projecting these trends into the future. His conjectures rest upon a very shaky implicit assumption that economic expansion and growth will continue to characterize the United States.

Although we also disagree with some other aspects of Glaser's discussion of social trends that have accompanied the societal movement toward increased modernization, we acknowledge that much of his commentary in Part II of his book on etiological forces in lawbreaking on the part of young males, and in Part III dealing with causal influences in violent crimes, victimless offenses, and adult property offender careers, is sensitive to the empirical evidence and of high quality. In these two major portions of his monograph, Glaser also proceeds to spell out a series of guidelines for criminal justice policy that flow out of the available theories and research evidence on offenders. Most of these policy guidelines take the following form:

> If you will at some future date wish to release offenders with minimum risk of their committing further crimes, do not set them apart from and out of communication with law-abiding persons any more than safety necessitates.[20]

> Maximize visiting of prisoners by outside persons of probable rehabilitative influence.[21]

> Commitment to criminality is increased if offenders perceive their treatment by a criminal justice agency as unjust and is diminished if they view their treatment as just.[22]

A number of these policy guidelines are relatively obvious and commonsensical rather than being very revealing or novel. Even so, there probably is something to be said for an explication of policy guidelines for dealing with offenders which grow out of careful examination of the existing research evidence. This monograph does a competent job of setting out a body of intervention principles, or what some others have termed *practice theory*.[23] *At the same time,*

---

[20] Ibid., p. 76.

[21] Ibid., p. 97.

[22] Ibid, p. 107.

[23] Ernest Greenwood, "Social Science and Social Work: A Theory of Their Relationship," *Social Service Review*, 29 (March 1955), 20–32.

the largest share of Glaser's material on policy guidelines is relatively
silent on the matter of allocation of resources and responsibilities
within the criminal justice system, which he identifies as the essence
of strategic planning at the beginning of his monograph. In short,
after enunciating the view that the introduction of *organizational*
innovations is the central task of justice planning, he then shifts to
a *client-centered* discussion of the kinds of intervention services to be
delivered to individual lawbreakers. By and large, his monograph
bears more than a slight similarity to an earlier attempt by Don
Gibbons to lay out practice principles structured upon behavioral
science evidence on criminality.[24] Whatever the merits of that kind
of discussion, it is more appropriately labeled as treatment theory
than as strategic planning theory.

Glaser is not entirely silent on the question of structural
change and justice planning. Thus at one point where he comments
upon the prevention of serious crime by adolescents, he offers the
following recommendations or principles:

Make school a less age-segregated and more gratifying, instructive,
and relevant experience for all students.

Link school more closely with employment.

Expand economic incentives to family cohesion and school atten-
dance by income maintenance and free school meal programs.

Abolish segregation of poor people in slums.[25]

These recommendations for changes in the schools, the world
of work, and slum conditions differ from the client-centered principles advanced by Glaser in earlier sections of his monograph. These
social-structural proposals call for large-scale efforts to rearrange the
organization of schools, youth employment, or urban structure, or
what many would term attacks upon the "root causes" of lawbreaking.
However, these proposals seem like throwaway lines, for Glaser has
little to say about how reforms in the schools or elsewhere might be
achieved. His statements are more in the nature of problem-defining
assertions than they are policy recommendations. In other words, an

---

[24] Don C. Gibbons, *Changing the Lawbreaker* (Englewood Cliffs, N.J.:
Prentice-Hall, 1965).

[25] Glaser, *Strategic Criminal Justice Planning*, pp. 114–19.

injunction to planners and others in the criminal justice field to abolish segregation identifies a broad goal but contains nothing in the way of specific direction on how to work toward that goal. Such injunctions share much in common with recommendations to prison guards that they "behave therapeutically" or to probation officers that they "make constructive use of authority." These guidelines are relatively vacuous ones unless we can also give guards or probation officers some more detailed advice on how to behave therapeutically or constructively.

We readily acknowledge that it is no small task to spell out plans by which significant organizational alterations can be brought about within the criminal justice apparatus or through which societal change might be effected. It would surely be unfair to criticize Glaser for not producing a detailed, grand design for organizational or societal change. At the same time, we need to keep the central planning goal in mind and not retreat to proposals for the delivery of correctional services to individual clients. We concur with Glaser that the criminal justice planning task ought to center on organizational and structural changes of the kind he hints at in his monograph. For the planner, the real challenge begins when he or she endeavors to move beyond the articulation of broad or general goals. For example, one might offer the view that offenders ought to be released from maximum security institutions to prerelease centers, rather than being dumped directly back into the free community. But if that is a planning goal, what then needs to be identified are the tactics through which legislative support for such centers can be marshaled, the stratagems and activities that can be utilized in order to "sell" a prerelease center to a particular urban neighborhood, and the coordinating steps that must be taken in order to introduce prerelease centers into the justice system without disrupting other parts of it.

Some other examples of the planning task have been enumerated in Chapter 2. For example, LEAA has recently embarked upon a funding program to support the diversion of youth from the juvenile justice machinery. That effort involved examination of questions centering on development of legal protections for diverted juveniles. The diversion planning also included scrutiny of alternative diversion program models or directions that could be pursued, such as youth advocacy programs as opposed to emphasis upon the delivery of services to individual divertees. Decisions also had to be reached regarding the stages within the justice machinery at which diversion is to occur. Then, too, attention was given to minimizing the possibility that these programs will "widen the nets" of the system because they will be utilized for petty offenders who would not have been inserted into the system at all in the absence of diversion programs. These constitute a sampling of the problems and tasks that had to be addressed in strategic or comprehensive planning for juvenile diversion.

Still another example of the dimensions of planning can be taken from the Multnomah County Jail, which is soon to be displaced by new freeway construction in Portland, Oregon. A whole host of issues center on funding of a new facility, architectural planning for that institution, decisions about the kinds of persons to be incarcerated there and the kinds of programs to be developed for them, and kindred other matters that will consume the time of a number of planners. Along the same line, a governor's task force and technical staff is currently engaged in comprehensive attempts to deal with rising prison populations in Oregon through alternative measures to building prisons, while some years earlier, much attention was centered on examination of the workings of county jails in Oregon, with an eye toward deciding whether state-operated regional jails should be constructed. A third illustration of planning problems can be found in the extensive study recently given to the possibility of consolidation of city and county police agencies in Multnomah County.[26]

To conclude these observations on Glaser's views, while he has emphasized the importance of strategic or innovative planning, his discussion of principles and procedures in strategic planning is somewhat brief and incomplete.

SUMMARY

This chapter has reviewed a number of conceptual frameworks and other relatively general discussions of justice planning that have been put forth to date. Our comments about the existing literature have been both appreciative and critical. On the one hand, we have suggested that statements offered by Frank and Faust, Glaser, and various other analysts are of considerable value in providing some indication of the parameters of the planning task. These essays also

---

[26] John E. Angell, Steven A. Egger, and Fontaine Hagedorn, *Staff Report: Police Consolidation Project* (Portland, Ore.: Police Consolidation Project, 1974).

offer a number of hints regarding significant planning concepts and some of the ingredients of the knowledge base upon which effective planning depends. On the whole, we have little disagreement with most of these ideas as they have to do with the proper focus for criminal justice planning efforts and related matters.

On the other hand, our major criticism of the material reviewed in this chapter is that most of it falls considerably short of providing us with detailed guidelines and resources that can be used in focused planning efforts. For example, most of these commentators have argued that the planner must be conversant with causal knowledge, data regarding the operation of justice system components, and planning concepts. However, most of these statements are relatively silent regarding the specific etiological generalizations that are most valid, specific propositions that emerge from the sociological analysis of the justice machinery, and the like.

We do not propose to offer a full-blown body of planning theory, a detailed compilation of core knowledge for planning, or a comprehensive statement of planning technology in this text. We do not think that one can move in one giant leap from the current state of affairs to outline the "last word" on criminal justice planning. However, the remaining chapters of this book will attempt to spell out a framework for criminal justice planning which draws upon the sources discussed to this point, but which also may advance the planning literature at least a modest step or two forward.

5

A Conceptual Framework for Planning: Core Knowledge

INTRODUCTION

All criminal justice planners would undoubtedly like to have at hand an abundance of knowledge, tools, and techniques to carry them through the tangled planning jungle of political interests, bureaucratic red tape, and ideological polarizations of planning participants and which would allow them to avoid the tension and conflict now inherent in the planning process. Except for some specific quantitative tools and some social interaction and problem-solving tactics, however, few critical planning principles are currently available. This is particularly the case for conceptual tools to employ in the difficult problem-identification, problem-solving, and decision-making processes of planning. What is available is a relatively limited grab bag of information, tools, tactics, and strategies that the planner must warp and bend to the tasks of the moment. Planning baseline knowledge and techniques, in other words, are not neatly collected into some comprehensive document from which they can be selected and applied to planning problems in a highly uniform, efficient, and productive manner. In Chapters 5 and 6 we present a partial supply of planning knowledge, principles, and guidelines which we believe has utility for justice planners, and in Chapter 7 we discuss some more specific instances of planning methodology.

Let us stipulate two points regarding our conception of planning, both of which were mentioned earlier in this book. *First, we agree with Glaser's emphasis upon strategic planning centered on the identification and implementation of alterations in organizational or societal arrangements, designed (a) to change in some way or another the responses made to offenders, or (b) to deal with the "root causes" of lawbreaking.*[1] Although we are also concerned about shorter-range allocative or tactical planning, we hold that much attention needs to be given to the development of strategic or comprehensive planning.

Second, strategic planning can occur at various governmental levels. For example, the federal government through LEAA engages in strategic or innovative planning when it encourages removal of status offenders from training schools or when federal emphasis is given to organizational innovations in police activities. Strategic planning should also be a continuing and important part of the state law enforcement planning agency that allocates block grant funds from LEAA; in addition, state correctional administrations engage in a variety of comprehensive planning activities. Then, too, justice planning can occur at the level of specific regions or jurisdictions within a state, such as when attention is given to improving the level of law enforcement and correctional activities within a standard metropolitan statistical area. Finally, planning takes place in specific justice agencies in the form of efforts to devise a new milieu program in a private child-care center, in planning for the construction of a new jail, or in reorganization of a police department.

So much for our conception of criminal justice planning. What kinds of knowledge and skill do planners need?

---

1 Daniel Glaser, *Strategic Criminal Justice Planning* (Rockville, Md.: National Institute of Mental Health, 1975), p. 4.

THE CORE ELEMENTS OF CRIMINAL
JUSTICE KNOWLEDGE

Suppose that we have encountered the compleat criminal justice planner. If such a person existed, he or she would be equipped with a wealth of information in each of the following categories.

First and foremost, effective criminal justice planning requires that the planner possess in-depth understanding of crime patterns, social forces in crime causation, key factors in the development of criminal careers, and kindred matters. The argument here is obvious enough, namely, that one can do relatively little in the way of planning for effective crime control or crime reduction measures in the absence of valid knowledge about the problem to be attacked. Analogies with medicine come quickly to mind, so that one can argue that just as effective medical practice depends upon a sophisticated grasp of biological facts, effective justice planning practice requires the practitioner to be steeped in the facts of criminality. Or, in much the same way, parallels can be drawn to urban planning, for nearly all would agree that competency in urban planning rests upon a solid grasp of generalizations from urban ecology, urban land economics, and other basic fields of knowledge.

Strategic planning also requires that a number of societal trends that impact upon crime be identified, anticipated, and incorporated into plans. These trends and changes include such things as shifts in the age structure of the population, developments in the economic sphere, and related social trends. The planner must be able to offer assessments of future trends in lawbreaking, which are in large part determined by broader societal changes. Glaser has put this point well:

> An understanding of criminal law changes can approach adequacy only if it takes account of developments in the total society, apart from the justice system. Thus an understanding of societal evolution in our time must be the basis for strategic criminal justice planning if it is to be effective in an age when all anticipations of specific crime rates and State practices must be tentative.[2]

---

[2] Ibid., p. 7. Parenthetically, we would also point out that comprehensive planning must be based to some considerable extent on forecasts of the directions

A second category of basic criminal justice planning knowledge is a detailed understanding of the criminal justice machinery in operation. Relatively abstract and metaphorical discussions of the sort that have been examined previously in this book, describing criminal justice as a system, do not provide the planner with sufficient appreciation of the complexities of the criminal justice apparatus.

Several groupings of information about the workings of the justice machinery can be identified. The first of these has to do with detailed facts regarding the overall criminal and juvenile justice organizational network and its "host" environment. The planner needs to understand such matters as the linkages of the justice operation with various "publics" and interest groups. It is not enough to note that legislators, the general public, and certain interest groups often have a stake in the governance of law enforcement, judicial, and correctional structures. What is also needed is extensive information that identifies the ways in which specific legislators, citizen groups, and other collections of persons exercise influence upon the system. The planner must be equipped with information about the decision-making structure of the community similar to the kind that Norton Long has identified for community processes more generally.[3] There is a vast body of theory and data on community power structure available to the planner;[4] unfortunately, little of the material on community power and decision making has dealt specifically with the criminal justice apparatus.

The importance of knowledge on decision processes is underscored by the almost total absence of commentary in the justice planning literature regarding the skill requirements necessary for plan implementation. It has only been in recent years, following the LEAA requirement of community involvement in planning, that justice agencies have had to give serious attention to community-related interests and to ways and means of participating with a much-expanded public. Justice planning now calls for skills in planning and plan implementation beyond those needed for survival in the relatively

that federal funding of criminal justice activities is likely to take in future years. Criminal justice programs are heavily influenced by changes in the direction in which the political winds are blowing.

[3] Norton Long, "The Local Community as an Ecology of Games," *American Journal of Sociology,* 6 (November 1958), 251–61.

[4] A comprehensive survey and evaluation of much of this material appears in John Walton, "Community Power and the Retreat From Politics: Full Circle after Twenty Years?" *Social Problems,* 23 (February 1976), 292–303.

contracted world of the past. But, again, the criminal justice literature offers little guidance as to how planners, administrators, judges, or practitioners can improve their ability to understand and deal with organizational and political forces or community attitudes and behavior. Criminal justice representatives will probably need to turn to allied sources such as land-use or environmental planning, planning administration, and social work literature for hints on linkages between planning theory and specific methods and skills that can be helpful in plan implementation.[5]

Another kind of baseline information regarding the workings of the justice system is needed as well. Detailed data are called for on the *internal* workings of the system and its individual components, so that the planner needs an in-depth appreciation of the existing evidence on such matters as the social organization of juvenile justice operations within a community, including the linkages of child welfare agencies to each other and to the court.[6] Fortunately, there is an impressive collection of evidence now at hand on such matters as the workings of prison communities, parole agencies, or other component parts of the justice system.[7] The planner can learn a good deal about the major interorganizational disagreements and value conflicts that make the justice machinery a nonsystem, and which stand in the way of innovative planning efforts, from this literature.

A final grouping of justice system information that is crucial in planning centers on the effects of correctional intervention activities upon offenders. The planner needs to know what program evaluation studies have shown to date regarding the impact (or lack of impact) of various intervention strategies. Although there are a number of summary reports of evaluation studies, as will be noted later in this book, those who have collated these program assessment studies do not all agree regarding the conclusions to be drawn from those experiments and quasi-experiments.

The third and final category of knowledge required by the compleat justice planner is a body of planning principles, concepts, and tools that can be utilized to deal with specific criminal justice

---

[5] For example, Jack Rothman, *Planning and Organizing for Social Change* (New York: Columbia University Press, 1974).

[6] For one example of this kind of information, see Robert M. Emerson, *Judging Delinquents* (Chicago: Aldine, 1969).

[7] Much of that data is reviewed in Don C. Gibbons, *Society, Crime, and Criminal Careers*, 3rd ed. (Englewood Cliffs, N.J.: Prentice-Hall, 1977), pp. 485–521.

planning problems. We have already seen in Chapter 4 that a number of persons have been groping toward the articulation of principles and tactics for justice planning, largely by borrowing from the established fields of social planning. Chapter 6 presents our own commentary on a conceptual foundation for justice planning, in which we also are involved in plundering the broader planning literature for potentially useful tools for justice planning.

SOME OBSERVATIONS ON CRIMINALITY AND CRIME CAUSATION

We began this chapter by arguing that the criminal justice planner ought to have a wealth of criminological knowledge regarding criminality and patterns of criminal behavior. Although we cannot provide a detailed presentation of criminological knowledge within the pages of this brief volume, we can outline some of the major facets of sociological wisdom regarding criminality.

Sociological Perspectives on Crime and Delinquency

It is a relatively easy task to identify a "mainstream" sociological viewpoint on the etiology of crime and delinquency, since it can be found in criminology textbooks and kindred sources. That sociological perspective attributes lawbreaking to a variety of "criminogenic" features, which are particularly pronounced in modern, urbanized and industrialized nations such as the United States. Then, too, sociological opinion holds that most offenders are psychologically normal individuals whose deviant behavior is the result of differential association, exposure to subcultural influences, or some parallel form of social learning. These core conclusions are contained in nearly all of the criminology textbooks that have been produced by sociologists in the past several decades. Moreover, these propositions are buttressed by a relatively abundant supply of empirical evidence that is also collated within criminology textbooks.

One systematic attempt to summarize the mainstream sociological perspective on criminality has been made by Don Gibbons. He sets forth seventeen propositions about which sociological consensus exists:

1. The members of a society are the carriers of an organization of social roles, that is, behavior patterns reflecting different social statuses or positions. (In other words, it is meaningful to approach the description of the behavior of individual persons by paying attention to the related but independent component activities or roles making up their behavior.)

2. Social roles are the product of social organization and socialization, that is, of the ongoing structure of society and of learning processes in primary groups. (In other words, the developmental process in human behavior centers around the acquisition, by the person, of a collection of social roles made available to him by the society in which he is found.)

3. Various patterns of social organization and socialization exist in complex societies so that, in turn, a variety of statuses and roles exist in them. There is a variety of nondeviant roles as well as a great many deviant ones (radical, homosexual, criminal, and so forth).

4. All people play criminal or delinquent roles at one time or another, if only symbolically. (In other words, petty violations of law are engaged in by nearly every person in the course of his lifetime. Also, many individuals entertain deviant and criminalistic motives but do not act upon them; thus they play deviant roles symbolically.)

5. Sociologically, "criminals" or "delinquents" are persons who play criminalistic roles heavily and/or who are identified by "society" as criminals or delinquents. (Persons who come to be tagged as offenders by the legal processes are frequently ones who are involved in repetitive and serious acts of law violation; but individuals who engage in petty and isolated acts of illegality are also sometimes reacted to as violators. Both of these groups are "criminals" or "delinquents" because they have been so labeled by the official machinery of social control.)

6. Criminal or delinquent behavior is one social role, but not

the only one, that persons play. Criminal or delinquent individuals also play roles as "citizen," "father," "employee," and so forth.

7. Among persons identified as criminals or delinquents, there are variations in the character and intensity of the deviant role. These include variations in both (a) actual deviant role behavior and (b) role-related social-psychological characteristics. The illegal acts carried on by offenders vary from one individual to another. Also, some persons have no self-image as a deviant, whereas others exhibit such self-definitions. In turn, among individuals with deviant or nondeviant self-conceptions, variations are exhibited in the particular kind of image held ("tough guy," "right guy," "smart hustler," and so on).

8. Stable patterns of criminal or delinquent roles, involving recurrent forms of deviant activity accompanied by uniform social-psychological role characteristics, can be observed in the population of offenders. In these terms, it can be said that types of criminalistic deviance exist.

9. Although behavioral and social-psychological changes occur in specific criminal or delinquent roles during the development of the role, these changes are limited, orderly, and identifiable. As a result, it is possible to define specific, stable criminal and delinquent role-careers. Offenders do not engage in random and unpredictable patterns of role-behavior; they do not "play the field" of offenses.

10. The specific etiological process that leads to one particular kind of criminalistic role behavior involves a number of causal variables and differs from that which produces another criminal role. In this sense, criminal and delinquent behavior is the product of multiple-causation. At the same time, it is possible to identify the different etiological processes which are implicated in the various forms of criminalistic deviance.

11. The learning of criminal and/or delinquent roles is maximized in a criminalistic society, and the United States is such a society.

12. Much, but not all, criminal and delinquent behavior in the competitive, materialistic American society is societally generated and takes the form of assaults upon property. Property

crime is not usually the expression of hidden motives but, rather, of surface ones. (Offenders steal to "make a living" rather than to commit symbolic incest and so on.)

13. Crime and delinquency in complex societies are encouraged in a variety of ways by that complexity. For example, police ineffectiveness is a correlate of a democratic, complex, urban social organization. In turn, ineffectual police work aids in the commission of crime and is an encouragement to criminality. (In a society which demands that law enforcement agents behave according to strict rules of arrest, search and seizure, interrogation, and the like, many offenders are inevitably going to avoid apprehension or conviction for crimes. Additionally, in a society in which relatively few policemen are employed to maintain surveillance over a large population living in metropolitan communities, the law enforcement persons are not going to be able to observe most illegal acts that occur. As a result, the risk of being apprehended for deviant acts will appear to be slight to many individuals.)

14. Some criminalistic roles are mainly the consequence of social-class variations in socialization and life experiences, along with other social-structural variables. In particular, situations in which legitimate avenues to the attainment of common American goals or values are blocked are importantly involved in certain forms of crime and delinquency.

15. Some criminalistic roles are produced by family and other socialization experiences which are not class-linked or class-specific. Among these are "parental rejection," "deviant sexual socialization," and others. These kinds of experiences occur at all social-class levels.

16. The "defining agencies" (police, probation services, courts, and so forth) play a part both in the definition of deviants and in the continuation of deviant roles. The result of apprehension and "treatment" may be quite contrary to the expected result. In other words, although one official function of correctional agencies and processes is the reformation of the offender, the actual outcome is often the isolation of the person, reinforcement of the deviant role, and rejection of society by the offender, the final result being nonreformation.

17. Variations can be seen in societal reactions to criminality of

different kinds. Personal offenses and crude, visible attacks upon property are likely to be severely dealt with and punitively handled. Accordingly, embezzlers and similar persons are reacted to differently than gas station stick-up artists or strong-arm robbers. In addition, societal reactions to criminal deviants are based upon other characteristics of the individual than criminal role behavior. Middle-class delinquents, for example, are accorded a societal reaction different from that directed toward working-class individuals involved in similar delinquent behavior. In turn, these reactions have implications for involvement in, and continuation in, criminality.[8]

Most of the pages of Gibbons's criminology textbook examine a large number of more specific hypotheses that flow out of these seventeen general propositions, along with a body of empirical evidence on offender patterns which has been produced to date. For example, semiprofessional property offenders are discussed at one point, with attention being focused on the offense patterns, social-psychological characteristics, and causal backgrounds of these offenders. At another point, naive check forgers are scrutinized and a body of evidence is presented regarding the personality characteristics, marital interaction patterns, and other characteristics of offenders who are involved in this pattern of lawbreaking. Other portions of that book are given over to detailed consideration of white-collar offenders, professional criminals, drug users, organized crime, sexual offenders, and a number of other patterns of criminality. We suggest that comprehensive textbooks such as this one by Gibbons represent basic sourcebooks for justice planners that are filled with a relatively rich storehouse of core knowledge for planning.

A parallel effort to capture the basic dimensions of the delinquency problem and the state of knowledge regarding the etiology of juvenile misconduct can be found in Gibbons's delinquency textbook.[9] In that work, over forty empirical propositions that emerge from the existing studies of delinquency are set forth. These generalizations are brought together in the concluding chapter of that book in the form of a propositional inventory containing assertions about (a) the extent of delinquency, (b) police and court handling of delin-

---

[8] Ibid., pp. 244–46.

[9] Don C. Gibbons, *Delinquent Behavior*, 2nd ed. (Englewood Cliffs, N.J.: Prentice-Hall, 1976).

quents, (c) role types in delinquency, (d) delinquency causation, and (e) the impact of correctional experiences upon offenders.[10] Although we do not have space here to present the entire propositional inventory, the flavor of that listing can be sensed from several examples:

> Hidden middle-class delinquency is widespread; nearly all middle income youths have committed at least a few acts which technically constitute delinquency. However, most hidden delinquency on the part of middle-class adolescents is relatively petty in form.

> Police dispositions tend to be related to demographic characteristics of offenders, thus males, blacks, lower income youths, and older boys are most frequently dealt with formally by court referral. These demographic characteristics enter into dispositions in part because males, older boys, blacks, and lower income youngsters appear to be disproportionately involved in serious, repetitive delinquencies. However, some studies have indicated that the police behave differently towards blacks, sending more of them to juvenile court than they do white youths involved in comparable offenses.

> Working-class boys become involved in subcultural misbehavior out of a variety of circumstances, but most of the causal influences center about social and economic deprivation experienced by lower income citizens in metropolitan neighborhoods. While there is no single route to involvement in subcultural delinquency, a set of related circumstances stemming from the social class structure conjoin to generate this behavior. Some gang offenders are responding to problems of perceived lack of opportunity and economic deprivation, others are more concerned about immediate status threats, still others are drawn into delinquency out of adjustment difficulties in school.

> "Under the roof" culture in the form of family tensions of one kind or another appears to be a major factor in female delinquency, although various social class factors and social liabilities apparently conjoin with parent-child relationships to push youngsters in the direction of delinquency involvement.

> Training schools apparently have benign effects upon wards processed through them; although "reformation" does not usually occur, neither does the institution directly contribute to recidivism.

---

[10] Ibid., pp. 285–92.

> Most training school wards emerge from these places with no more criminal skills or more serious antisocial attitudes than when they entered.

As in the criminology textbook, Gibbons's delinquency volume contains a large collection of research findings from various studies of juvenile lawbreaking. The justice planner can learn much about various patterns of delinquency in American society from this collation of the existing evidence. On this point, it might be noted that many of the propositions about juvenile delinquency that are found in *Delinquent Behavior* were incorporated into the theoretical rationale for the LEAA-funded national effort in juvenile diversion, inaugurated in 1976.[11]

Continuing Quarrels Regarding Crime Causation

We do not wish to mislead the reader regarding sociological perspectives on crime, delinquency, and etiological processes. Complete unanimity of opinion does not exist on all of the details of lawbreaking and its causes. Rather, consensus on causal issues begins to break down somewhat as soon as attention turns to more specific causal propositions. A number of observers have pointed out that individual sociologists differ significantly from each other in terms of the more specific theoretical positions to which they hold allegiance.[12] Thus, on the question of social-structural forces in lawbreaking, some sociologists stress theories revolving around assumptions that a set of core values exists in the United States, with those persons who are cut off from access to those values being most likely to suffer from *anomie* and most vulnerable to involvement in deviance and criminality. Others eschew the view that core values can be identified, opting instead for arguments stressing value-pluralism and value-conflicts as primary forces in criminality.

---

[11] Law Enforcement Assistance Administration, *Program Announcement: Diversion of Youth from the Juvenile Justice System* (Washington, D.C.: Office of Juvenile Justice and Delinquency Prevention, April 1976).

[12] Theories on the causes of deviance and criminality are examined in detail in Don C. Gibbons and Joseph F. Jones, *The Study of Deviance* (Englewood Cliffs, N.J.: Prentice-Hall, 1975); also see Gibbons, *Society, Crime, and Criminal Careers;* and Gibbons, *Delinquent Behavior.*

Contemporary sociologists also disagree on the more specific question of the socialization and other social experiences involved in the acquisition of patterns of deviant behavior by specific individuals. Some emphasize social learning views such as Sutherland's theory of differential association,[13] which contends that persons acquire motivational patterns favoring lawbreaking through social learning experiences. Others stress a social control position that does not posit any special motivation toward deviance; rather, it argues that persons are likely to engage in deviance whenever the social ties that bind them to the moral order are broken.[14] Still another group of sociologists has been highly vocal in recent years in advancing social reaction or labeling notions that suggest that deviant careers—that is, persistent involvement in lawbreaking—are often produced by those correctional responses directed at deviants that are supposed to lead them out of lawbreaking.

Space limitations prevent examination of the various positions taken by sociologists on the question of causation. But enough has been said to demonstrate that complete unanimity of opinion on questions of etiology does not exist. Moreover, it would be naive to suppose that sociological harmony on these issues will develop in the near future, as soon as adequate empirical evidence is forthcoming.[15] For one thing, the multicausal nature of criminality means that the explanatory task will always be one of trying to identify the *relative*

---

[13] Edwin H. Sutherland and Donald R. Cressey, *Principles of Criminology*, 9th ed. (Philadelphia: Lippincott, 1974), pp. 75–77.

[14] These different views are discussed in Gibbons and Jones, *Study of Deviance*, pp. 122–41.

[15] Although discussion of this point would take us too far afield, it ought to be noted in passing that probably the most fundamental problem preventing sociologists from reaching nearly complete agreement on "the facts" concerning criminality has to do with the logical and structural deficiencies of sociological theorizing. Discussions of the logical shortcomings of sociological theories can be found in Charles W. Lachenmeyer, *The Language of Sociology* (New York: Columbia University Press, 1971); Jack P. Gibbs, *Sociological Theory Construction* (Hinsdale, Ill.: Dryden Press, 1972); and Clarence Schrag, "Elements of Theoretical Analysis in Sociology," in Llewellyn Gross, ed., *Sociological Theory: Inquiries and Paradigms* (New York: Harper & Row, 1967), pp. 220–53. The thrust of the observations by these writers is that sociological concepts and formulations are often so fuzzy and ambiguous that sociologists literally do not know what they are talking about, that is, they exhibit little or no agreement on the empirical indicators of such notions as "anomie" and "opportunity structures." This gap between theoretical concepts and specific research observations has much to do with accounting for the interminable argumentation that appears in the social science literature regarding the extent to which the data do or do not support some particular hypothesis or theory.

significance of one factor or another as it operates in some complex causal mixture with myriad other factors. Also, judgments about the degree of importance to be attached to one explanatory variable or another will continue to be equivocal and subject to challenge because these assertions will always be drawn out of studies of some sample of offenders in some specific locale, rather than from a comprehensive empirical study of all lawbreakers.

The thrust of these remarks is that criminology textbooks and practice theory statements such as Gibbons's *Changing the Lawbreaker* or Glaser's *Strategic Criminal Justice Planning*, which endeavor to spell out implications of causal knowledge for correctional intervention purposes, must be viewed as judicious attempts to weigh and evaluate the existing empirical evidence. Many of the claims advanced in them are subject to challenge.[16]

---

[16] One point of particular importance concerns the matter of diagnostic typologies as a basis for criminal justice planning. Although offender classifications are of considerable utility in planning, we need to note that these typologies present a somewhat distorted picture of the real world, in that they characterize offender roles as more fixed and clear-cut than they often are in fact. This point has been made by Glaser, *Adult Crime and Social Policy* (Englewood Cliffs, N.J.: Prentice-Hall, 1972), p. 14: "In the real world, the gradation and mixtures of characteristics in people are so extensive that most of our categories must be given very arbitrary boundaries if everyone in a cross-section of the population is to be placed in one empirical type or another. Most real people just do not fall neatly into uniform patterns. Therefore, we formulate explanations in terms of idealizations, we revise them on the basis of research on empirical types, and in the practical world we qualify most explanations for separate cases to meet the variations we encounter beyond what any set of type labels denote." Parallel observations on typologies have been made in Don C. Gibbons, "Offender Typologies—Two Decades Later," *British Journal of Criminology*, 15 (April 1975), 140–56.

Confusion on the question of causation is compounded by the fact that other voices can be heard in this babble of conflicting testimony, so that psychologists and psychiatrists frequently come forth to assert other, quite different, claims about etiology from those by sociologists. For example, much attention has focused in recent years upon the interpersonal maturity levels theory employed in the Community Treatment Project in California.

The interpersonal maturity levels argument and the Community Treatment Project are described in Ted Palmer, "The Youth Authority's Community Treatment Project," *Federal Probation*, 38 (March 1974), 3–14. For critical comments on the maturity levels theory and the treatment project, see Don C. Gibbons, "Differential Treatment of Delinquents and Interpersonal Maturity Levels Theory: A Critique," *Social Service Review*, 44 (March 1970), 22–33; Jerome Beker and Doris S. Heyman, "A Critical Evaluation of the California Differential Treatment Typology of Adolescent Offenders," *Criminology*, 10 (May 1972), 3–59; and Paul Lerman, "Evaluative Studies of Institutions for Delinquents: Implications for Research and Social Policy," *Social Work*, 13 (July 1968), 55–64.

Our position on etiological knowledge comes down to this: no single body of causal theory now in existence is unequivocally supported by an abundance of solid empirical evidence. Most of the propositions about criminality and causation to be derived from the criminological literature must be qualified, so that we must speak in terms of moderately significant correlations and the like. Even so, some etiological hypotheses show greater validity than do others. It is incumbent upon criminologists, criminal justice planners, and others who would employ these theories and findings to do so judiciously by becoming methodologically sophisticated enough to evaluate the claims and findings of criminological inquiry.[17] Finally, nothing that we have said about the deficiencies of core knowledge regarding criminality ought to be interpreted as a recommendation for the abandonment of theorizing and research evidence as a basis for justice planning. Tactical or strategic planning worthy of those designations must be based on a considered assessment of etiological forces in lawbreaking, even though some degree of uncertainty about the causal underpinnings of criminal justice ventures will continue to be inevitable.[18]

This case of psychopathological theories of delinquency such as the interpersonal maturity levels is one where, in our opinion, the facts are relatively clear and unequivocal. The mass of evidence from many studies of psychological characteristics on the part of delinquents does not lend support to psychogenic formulations, including the I-Levels argument. See Gibbons, *Delinquent Behavior*, pp. 74–89. Also, the critics have pointed to a number of defects in the Community Treatment Project data which supporters of this argument have adduced in support of it. See Beker and Heyman, "Critical Evaluation"; and Gibbons, "Differential Treatment of Delinquents and Interpersonal Maturity Levels Theory."

[17] One useful guidebook for evaluation of criminological research findings is Travis Hirschi and Hanan C. Selvin, *Delinquency Research: An Appraisal of Analytic Methods* (New York: Free Press, 1967).

[18] These remarks should not be interpreted as a rejection of *offense-based* planning, as opposed to *offender-based* efforts. For one example of a discussion of crime-control strategies centered on offense information rather than offender characteristics, see Thomas A. Reppetto, "Crime Prevention and the Displacement Phenomenon," *Crime and Delinquency*, 22 (April 1976), 166–77.

Along this same line, the planner ought to draw upon research findings on such matters as crime reduction through such policies as intensified police control. A complex experiment in Kansas City, Missouri, has cast some doubt upon the traditional police view that intensified police patrol in urban neighborhoods will decrease opportunities for crime and increase the arrest rates for reported crimes. See George L. Kelling, Tony Pate, Duane Dieckman, and Charles E. Brown, *The Kansas City Preventive Patrol Experiment: A Summary Report* (Washington, D.C.: Police Foundation, 1974). The authors of this report indicate that (p. 1): "Three controlled levels of

Causal Perspectives and Justice Planning:
Some Examples

All programs designed to control or curb lawbreaking are based upon some version or another of causal argument, although in many cases the etiological perspectives upon which efforts are based are implicit rather than explicit. Then, too, it is relatively easy to identify crime control or intervention endeavors that have been predicated upon invalid notions of causation. Nonetheless, the basic point remains—there are no crime control measures that do not ultimately rest upon some perspective regarding the sources or causes of lawbreaking.

Attempts to develop structured responses to criminality that grow out of an explicit, detailed theoretical rationale are a relatively recent development. In the last decade or so, many ventures of this kind have been launched, particularly in the correctional segment of the criminal justice apparatus. These theoretically informed programs stand as illustrations of the kind of planned efforts that are sorely needed if the crime problem is to be dented. Let us examine a few of these planned projects.

---

routine police preventive patrol were used in the experimental areas. One area, termed 'reactive,' received no preventive patrol. Officers entered the area only in response to citizen calls for assistance. This in effect substantially reduced police visibility in the area. In the second area, called 'proactive,' police visibility was increased two to three times its usual level. In the third area, termed 'control,' the normal level of patrol was maintained. Analysis of the data gathered revealed that the three areas experienced no significant differences in the level of crime, citizens' attitudes toward police services, citizens' fear of crime, police response time, or citizens' satisfaction with police response time."

However, some others have examined the data from the Kansas City experiment and have noted that the patrol intensity variations actually experienced in these areas were not marked during the experimental period, so that considerable doubt is cast upon the conclusions of this study. See Richard C. Larson, "What Happened to Patrol Operations in Kansas City? A Review of the Kansas City Preventive Patrol Experiment," *Journal of Criminal Justice*, 3 (Winter 1975), 267–97. For a more general discussion of the issue of crime control through increased police surveillance, see James P. Levine, "The Ineffectiveness of Adding Police to Prevent Crime," *Public Policy*, 4 (Fall 1975), 523–45.

Finally, on the matter of crime control measures that are centered on crime patterns rather than on offenders, the planner might examine the environmental design proposals of Newman. See Oscar Newman, *Defensible Space* (New York: Macmillan, 1972); and Newman, *Design Guidelines for Creating Defensible Space* (Washington, D.C.: Law Enforcement Assistance Administration, 1976).

The C-Unit Project was conducted at Deuel Vocational Institution in California in the 1960s.[19] This program attempted to develop a social community among inmates and staff in one living unit in that institution, with the hope that a common moral code would develop to regularize social interaction among members. Further, this therapeutic milieu program was intended to produce law-abiding behavior on the part of inmates when they were released from prison. In their report on this project, the authors indicated that it was based on four basic assumptions about offenders:

1. Imprisoned offenders are like other people in desiring to walk with dignity among their fellows, to give as well as to receive, and to behave as responsible members of a community. Under conditions that support the expression of these desires in behavior, most offenders reveal some capacity to act accordingly.

2. Men who have the opportunity to act as responsible community members during their stay in prison should be better able on release to meet the expectations of the free community. At the least, a life in prison that encourages an inmate to exercise the social competence of which he is capable will do minimal harm to his readiness to behave responsibly; at best, such an experience will increase the inmate's ability to perform consistently within the community's basic moral code.

3. Most offenders experience the sequence of offense, arrest, interrogation, detention, adjudication, and imprisonment as a major life crisis that disrupts accustomed adaptations and requires some sort of reorganization of the self in relation to society. Like other persons in crisis, most offenders can use assistance in making constructive adaptations, the kind of help needed depending on their problems, resources, and goals. The help indicated may range from fairly simple human supports through various kinds of skill training to complicated therapies. What help is appropriate for which inmates can most be economically determined under conditions that encourage each person to act in the present at the top of his social capacity.

---

[19] Elliot Studt, Sheldon L. Messinger, and Thomas P. Wilson, *C-Unit: Search for Community in Prison* (New York: Russell Sage, 1968).

4. Prison inmates, like other people, make effective use of proffered help only as they act on their immediate reality. The
inmates do the work of preparing themselves for membership
in the free community or it does not get done; official helpers
can only encourage and influence the direction of learning,
growth, and change. Conditions that support any person in
efforts to improve his social performance include: recognition
of his essential contribution to the task, encouragement to
work with others in the achievement of common goals, opportunities to come to grips with problems like those he will
be expected to meet in the future, and training in problem-
solving skills.[20]

The architects of this project, operating in terms of these assumptions, went about a detailed process of planning for the creation
of a therapeutic milieu program within the C-Unit dormitory. Unfortunately, they were not able to fully implement their plan due to
the unwillingness, inability, or both, of the prison staff and the statewide organization to engage in the reciprocal adjustments and change
required for planned innovations to succeed.

Another project that was built upon a detailed and explicit
theoretical rationale was the Provo Experiment conducted in Provo,
Utah.[21] The causal perspective on which that endeavor was based
argued that court-processed serious delinquents are usually from
lower-income homes, are characterized by failure in school and in the
world of work, and join delinquent groups in order to attain social,
emotional, and economic goals not otherwise available to them. One
of the principal designers of that project, LaMar Empey, has summarized the intervention program that grew out of this causal argument which we have only sketched here:

Postulates for intervention, therefore, suggested that a program
should try: (1) to make the delinquent group the target of change—
that is, attempt to change shared standards, points of view, re-
wards, and punishments; (2) to give the delinquent group a stake in

20 Ibid., p. 4.

21 The Provo Experiment is described in LaMar T. Empey, *Alternatives to
Incarceration* (Washington, D.C.: Department of Health, Education, and Welfare,
1967); Empey and Maynard L. Erickson, *The Provo Experiment: Impact and Death of
an Innovation* (Lexington, Mass.: Lexington Books, 1972).

what happens to its members by permitting participation with staff in solving problems, exerting controls, and making basic decisions; and (3) to open up conventional opportunities to delinquents in the school, the world of work, and other conventional institutions.[22]

Many other correctional intervention programs constructed upon explicit and detailed causal theories could be listed.[23] Examples of law enforcement activities that are undergirded by explicitly stated causal arguments are less numerous, but one can point to such efforts as the Kansas City Preventive Patrol Experiment as illustrative of the link between etiological arguments and crime control proposals.[24] That endeavor, along with others such as a program of intensified street lighting being conducted in Portland, Oregon, involves a number of assumptions about the character of garden-variety predatory street crime. These efforts rest upon characterizations that stress the rational but opportunistic nature of this behavior, and they assume that those who engage in it will be less likely to do so if it is made more risky through intensified police patrol or increased street illumination. Similar assumptions are contained in traffic enforcement tactics involving the posting of highway signs warning motorists that the roads are patrolled by radar or in the posting of warnings against shoplifting in department stores.

ON THE IMPACT OF CORRECTIONAL TREATMENT PROGRAMS

From the turn of the century until relatively recently, there has been considerable criminological enthusiasm as well as public support for correctional treatment. Sociologists have often been in the forefront

[22] Empey, *Alternatives to Incarceration*, p. 38. Empey has been involved in another complex intervention project constructed on a detailed, empirically based, sociological theory of delinquency. See LaMar T. Empey and Steven G. Lubeck, *The Silverlake Experiment* (Chicago: Aldine, 1971).

[23] For summaries of many of these programs, see Gibbons, *Society, Crime, and Criminal Careers*, pp. 523–51; and Gibbons, *Delinquent Behavior*, pp. 251–83.

[24] Kelling, Pate, Dieckman, and Brown, *Kansas City Preventive Control Experiment*. See footnote 18.

of the rehabilitation movement, agitating for more professional treatment workers, expansion of parole and other services, and improvements in the "treatment theory" on which correctional ventures are based.[25] In the past decade, however, much pessimism has developed regarding the prospects for correctional treatment. Disillusionment with the treatment goal has been voiced by many observers of the contemporary scene. Probably the most influential of these statements is that of James Q. Wilson, arguing for a return to emphasis upon deterrence and incapacitation of offenders, particularly through increasing both the certainty and the severity of punishment.[26]

Those who contend that criminal justice responses to offenders ought to move in the direction of deterrence models, stressing swift, certain, and perhaps severe punishments inflicted upon offenders, stand upon very shaky ground as far as supporting empirical evidence for those recommendations is concerned. Although these neoconservative deterrence proposals have captured the attention of many citizens, it is relatively easy to determine the flimsiness of the evidence on which they rest.[27]

But, unfortunately for the person who would offer positive counterproposals to those recommendations of the deterrence advocates, one can find little firm evidence pointing to any significant im-

---

[25] Examples of this kind are Don C. Gibbons, *Changing the Lawbreaker* (Englewood Cliffs, N.J.: Prentice-Hall, 1965); and Glaser, *Strategic Criminal Justice Planning;* and *Adult Crime and Social Policy.*

[26] James Q. Wilson, *Thinking about Crime* (New York: Basic Books, 1975). For a severe but reasoned criticism of Wilson's arguments, see Jerome H. Skolnick, "Are More Jails the Answer?" *Dissent,* 23 (Winter 1976), 95–97. Another hard-line statement is Ernest Van den Haag, *Punishing Criminals: Concerning a Very Old and Painful Question* (New York: Basic Books, 1975).

[27] The complexity of the deterrence question is indicated in Jack P. Gibbs, *Crime, Punishment, and Deterrence* (New York: Elsevier, 1975). The central thrust of Gibbs's book is that the phenomenon of deterrence is so much bound up with other factors and with other consequences of punishment as to be almost beyond empirical investigation. At the very least, his discussion indicates that almost nothing can be asserted unequivocally about deterrence on the basis of the research evidence at hand. For other summaries of the existing research on deterrence, see Charles W. Thomas and J. Sherwood Williams, eds., *The Deterrent Effect of Sanctions: A Selected Bibliography* (Metropolitan Criminal Justice Center, College of William and Mary, 1975); Charles R. Tittle and Charles H. Logan, "Sanctions and Deviance: Evidence and Remaining Questions," *Law and Society Review,* 8 (Spring 1973), 371–92; and Franklin Zimring and Gordon J. Hawkins, *Deterrence: The Legal Threat in Crime Control* (Chicago: University of Chicago Press, 1973).

pact that therapeutic intervention has upon lawbreakers.[28] Most of the available data suggest that whatever the results of various dispositions such as probation or imprisonment upon offenders, these outcomes are explained more by the background characteristics of the persons who succeed or fail in these structures than by the therapeutic actions directed at them.[29]

Evidence on Treatment Impact

One pessimistic review of correctional treatment endeavors has been presented by Walter Bailey, who examined one hundred studies of correctional outcome published between 1940 and 1960.[30] About two-thirds of the programs were based on a "sick" model of the offender, who was in need of psychotherapeutic handling. Bailey drew the following conclusion from these studies:

> Since positive results were indicated in roughly one-half of the total sample of 100 reports analyzed, the problem of interpretation is not unrelated to that of determining "whether the cup is half empty or half full." But, when one recalls that these results, in terms of success or failure of the treatment used, are based upon the conclusions of the authors of the reports, themselves, then the implications of these findings regarding the effectiveness of correctional treatment become rather discouraging. A critical evaluation of the actual design and the specific research procedures described in each instance would substantially decrease the relative frequency of successful outcomes based upon reliably valid evidence. *Therefore, it seems quite clear that, on the sample of outcome reports with all of its limitations, evidence supporting the efficacy of correctional treatment is slight, inconsistent, and of questionable reliability* (emphasis added).[31]

---

[28] The evidence on the impact of correctional experiences upon offenders is examined at length in Gibbons, *Society, Crime, and Criminal Careers.*

[29] Stanton Wheeler, "Socialization in Correctional Institutions," in David A. Goslin, ed., *Handbook of Socialization Theory and Research* (Chicago: Rand McNally, 1969), pp. 1005–23.

[30] Walter C. Bailey, "An Evaluation of 100 Studies of Correctional Outcome," *Journal of Criminal Law, Criminology and Police Science,* 57 (June 1966), 153–60.

[31] Ibid., p. 158.

Another of these negative assessments of treatment is contained in an examination by Robison and Smith of about a dozen projects carried on in California.[32] They employed the studies in an attempt to gauge whether different posttreatment outcomes might be produced by sentencing persons to probation rather than imprisonment, by varying the length of the period of incarceration, by different forms of treatment in the institution, by variations in the intensity of probation or parole supervision, or by releasing persons to parole as contrasted to discharging them outright from prison. Robison and Smith concluded that any variations in outcomes observed for these different dispositions were the result either of initial differences among the types of offenders processed by community agencies or institutions or of variations in agency policies, rather than being due to treatment impact. For example, they noted that the seemingly more positive impact of the Community Treatment Project was a reflection of more lenient revocation policies on the part of parole agents supervising the experimental group cases.

One conclusion drawn by Robison and Smith regarding the question of long prison sentences as a means of curtailing crime is well worth repeating:

> It is difficult to escape the conclusion that the act of incarcerating a person at all will impair whatever potential he has for crime-free future adjustment and that, regardless of which "treatments" are administered while he is in prison, the longer he is kept there the more he will deteriorate and the more likely it is that he will recidivate. In any event, it seems almost certain that releasing men from prison earlier than is now customary in California would not increase recidivism.[33]

The most ambitious and devastating of these surveys of correctional intervention results is the study made by Douglas Lipton, Robert Martinson, and Judith Wilks.[34] They examined 231 treatment

---

[32] James Robison and Gerald Smith, "The Effectiveness of Correctional Programs," *Crime and Delinquency*, 17 (January 1971), 67–80.

[33] Ibid., p. 72.

[34] Douglas Lipton, Robert Martinson, and Judith Wilks, *The Effectiveness of Correctional Treatment—A Survey of Treatment Evaluation Studies* (Springfield, Mass.: Praeger, 1975); and Martinson, "What Works?—Questions and Answers about Prison Reform," *Public Interest*, 35 (Spring 1974), 22–54.

projects that had been conducted between 1945 and 1967, categorized in terms of the treatment methods employed, such as milieu therapy, parole supervision, medical treatment, individual counseling, and group therapy. Treatment outcomes were examined in a number of different ways, including recidivism, personality and attitude change, and community adjustment. The central conclusion from this massive scrutiny of treatment ventures was that *"with few and isolated exceptions, the rehabilitative efforts that have been reported so far have had no appreciable effect on recidivism"* (emphasis in original).[35]

Some Dissenting Views

There have been other voices raised in this chorus of pessimism about correctional intervention.[36] Even so, some continue to see a ray of hope for correctional treatment contained within these generally negative studies. For example, Charles Shireman, Katherine Mann, Charles Larsen, and Thomas Young reviewed a dozen studies of treatment within correctional institutions.[37] They concluded that certain forms of institutional therapy may produce results sufficiently powerful to carry over into the postrelease period, such as short-term milieu therapy coupled with a situation of high staff morale. Also, they found some indication in the twelve projects that intensive milieu treatment directed at younger boys, group counseling of young first offenders, certain kinds of individual psychiatric therapy given to younger adolescents, and provision of plastic surgery to selected cases all are associated with positive treatment results.

Daniel Glaser has examined a number of correctional treatment studies and has presented a similar argument to the effect that

---

[35] Martinson, "What Works?" p. 25.

[36] For example, see David A. Ward, "Evaluative Research for Corrections," in Lloyd E. Ohlin, ed., *Prisoners in America* (Englewood Cliffs, N.J.: Prentice-Hall, 1973), pp. 184–203; and Don C. Gibbons and Gerald F. Blake, "Evaluating the Impact of Juvenile Diversion Programs," *Crime and Delinquency*, 22 (October 1976), 411–20. Gibbons and Blake reviewed a dozen juvenile diversion projects and reported that most of them were deficient in terms of research design. Also, little evidence of greater success attributable to diversion as opposed to more conventional processing of youthful offenders could be found in these projects.

[37] Charles H. Shireman, Katherine Baird Mann, Charles Larsen, and Thomas Young, "Findings from Experiments in Treatment in the Correctional Institution," *Social Service Review*, 46 (March 1972), 38–59.

certain programs appear to work for certain kinds of offenders.[38] Both
in the PICO (Pilot Intensive Counseling Organization) project in a
California prison, involving intensive counseling administered to inmates,[39] and in the Community Treatment Project, some evidence
points to the positive impact of counseling upon offenders variously
classified as "conflicted," "neurotic," or "amenable" to treatment.
Finally, Ted Palmer has observed that Martinson's report on the effectiveness of correctional intervention contains some supporting evidence for the argument that certain specific tactics of treatment are
associated with significant posttreatment results.[40]

As we move into the last quarter of the twentieth century, it
is not clear what the final result will be of the current dialogue on correctional intervention. However, it seems probable that efforts to rehabilitate offenders will continue for some time, if for no other reason
than inertia. There have been several decades of development of the
treatment goal, resulting in generous amounts of public funds being
expended on correctional intervention and the creation of a massive
correctional bureaucracy. Once in operation, it is difficult to bring
this machinery to a halt.

The authors of this book contend that correctional treatment
has not yet had a complete and fair trial. At the same time, it is likely
that intervention efforts will need to move away from many of those
earlier stratagems that were based on psychiatric images of offenders
and on efforts to tinker with their mental health through some kind
of individual counseling or therapy. Treatment endeavors of the future are going to require more attention to *posttreatment contingen-
cies*, such as possession of a worthwhile job and availability of advanced educational opportunities, which play a major part in success
or failure. Intervention activities in the coming decades will probably
be more concerned with increasing the offender's "stake in conformity." It is necessary to recognize, however, that provision of chal-
lenging occupational opportunities and kindred efforts are much easier

---

[38] Glaser, *Strategic Criminal Justice Planning*, pp. 92–94.

[39] Stuart Adams, "The PICO Project," in Norman Johnston, Leonard Savitz,
and Marvin E. Wolfgang, eds., *The Sociology of Punishment and Corrections*, 2nd ed.
(New York: John Wiley, 1970), pp. 548–61.

[40] Ted Palmer, "Martinson Revisited," *Journal of Research in Crime and
Delinquency*, 12 (July 1975), 133–52. Also see Charles H. Logan, "Evaluation Research in Crime and Delinquency: A Reappraisal," *Journal of Criminal Law, Criminology and Police Science*, 63 (September 1972), 378–87.

to identify than to accomplish. The prospects for major reforms in the economic order and occupational structure of the United States do not seem promising at a time when the economic health of the nation seems to be moving toward a relatively permanent state of debilitation.

In this section, we have done little more than hint at some of the gaps and ambiguities in the available evidence regarding correctional intervention within the justice system. But enough has been said to indicate that correctional and criminal justice planning require that the planner have a sound grasp of the discordant findings that have emerged to date, so that he or she can make the wisest possible decisions about the most profitable directions to pursue in the effort to increase the impact of correctional intervention. The planning task surely is one that will call for hard thinking about issues for which the existing evidence provides only tentative answers at best.

SUMMARY

This chapter presented a series of our own observations about the elements of the knowledge base on which comprehensive and realistic planning depends. We have stressed the importance of sociological knowledge in justice planning, in large part because sociologists have been more systematically engaged in the study of crime and responses to it than have the members of other social science disciplines. However, we suggest that justice planning might also be strengthened by the research work now being done by political scientists and economists, some of which we have alluded to in these pages.[41] Then, too,

---

[41] Much of the economic literature on criminality involves rather complex mathematical techniques of one kind or another, as well as some tenuous assumptions about offender behavior. For a small sampling of this research literature, see Gary Becker, "Crime and Punishment: An Economic Approach," *Journal of Political Economy,* 76 (March–April, 1968), 169–217; and Sheldon Danziger and David Wheeler, "The Economics of Crime: Punishment or Income Redistribution," *Review of Social Economy,* 33 (October 1975), 113–30. This second essay centers on the concept of utility maximization, arguing that individuals engage in criminality in order to maximize profit or income to themselves. More important, these authors present an argument close to those offered by sociologists. They maintain that lawbreaking is a response to perceptions of *relative inequality* on the part of offenders, rather than to absolute inequality. Their notion of relative inequality parallels the sociological concept of relative deprivation. Danziger and Wheeler argue that offenders gauge relative inequality by comparing themselves with various reference groups.

although geographers, anthropologists, and historians have had little to say about criminological matters, these scholars have the potential for contributing significantly to the understanding of criminality and ultimately to planning and crime control.[42]

Our remarks so far have had relatively little to do with either the planning process itself or planning techniques and methodology. It is time now to turn to planning technology. Chapter 6 spells out a framework for criminal justice planning, drawing upon the sources discussed to this point and, most importantly, from a body of conceptual contributions that have been made in the broad area of social planning.

Finally, they provide evidence from a large sample of American cities, indicating that rising crime rates in the United States in the 1960s accompanied a situation in which general economic growth took place, but with a constant distribution of income. Stated differently, although economic growth was prominent during this period, the relative economic position of the disadvantaged did not improve, which may have given rise to heightened perceptions of relative inequality or deprivation on their part.

[42] For one indication of the directions geographic analysis might take, see Keith D. Harries, *The Geography of Crime and Justice* (New York: McGraw-Hill, 1974). Two valuable historical analyses are David J. Rothman, *Discovery of the Asylum* (Boston: Little, Brown, 1971); and Robert M. Mennel, *Thorns and Thistles* (Hanover, N.H.: The University Press of New England, 1973).

6

A Conceptual
Framework
for Planning:
Planning Principles

INTRODUCTION

Having come this far in this book, we have already revealed many
elements of our conceptual perspective on criminal justice planning.
We have made it abundantly clear that we are vigorous exponents of
planning, so that although Chapter 3 identified a number of obstacles
to planning, we regard these as problems to be overcome and not as
reasons for abandoning the cause of planning.

A fundamental roadblock to justice planning is that the
notion that this apparatus constitutes a system is more a crude meta-
phor than it is an accurate description of reality. At the same time,
we have emphasized throughout the preceding pages that we agree
with those who have argued that justice planning must be *system
oriented* and attuned to the consequences of actions taken at one

point in the machinery for operations someplace else in the structure.

In Chapter 3 we indicated that we concur with those planning theorists who have argued for *incremental planning* in criminal justice, in which plans are evolved, implemented, evaluated, and ultimately revised, in a continuing process. Although we also favor the development of comprehensive plans, we are relatively unenthusiastic about sterile forms of "master planning," in which someone goes about devising a "grand design" for the justice system of the future, with little or no concern for implementation of that design or for revisions of it in the light of new social developments.

Although we regard incremental planning as offering more promise than "master planning" or the alternative of postponing planning efforts until more research evidence has accumulated, this opinion ought not to be interpreted as advocacy of maintenance of the status quo. We emphatically disagree with those who would equate "projecting"—that is, the simple extension of existing programs a year or two into the future—with planning. Moreover, we indicated in Chapter 4 that we favor major emphasis upon "strategic" or "innovative" planning centered on system change, as contrasted to "tactical" or "allocative" planning which is concerned with resource distribution among existing programs.

A final point has already been introduced regarding our perspective. We view planning as a process that can and does occur on a variety of levels, ranging from local criminal justice networks, through state systems, to planning on the federal level. It is now time to take up, in more detail, some of the issues summarized above, in order to put forth the elements of our theoretical framework somewhat more systematically.

PLANNING THEORY

A central thesis of this book is that criminal justice planning is a relatively feeble, immature form of planning practice that lacks a rich body of sophisticated planning theory. We have advised neophyte justice planners to turn to the literature in the broader field of social planning for some useful concepts, generalizations, and principles, and we have also noted some of these potentially useful theoretical elements in earlier pages.

There is only a meager supply of criminal justice planning

theory, but the same is not true for the broader field of social planning. There is a voluminous and variegated accumulation of theory upon which justice planners can draw, so much so that our task is the difficult one of sorting and sifting through this material. We cannot turn to a single compendium of the collected wisdom of social planners from which we can borrow. Additionally, the social planning literature is so large, complex, and diverse that it is not possible to reduce it to a few brief pages. The following paragraphs present an overview of social planning theory, principally in order to titillate the reader's curiosity. Stated another way, these paragraphs open a window upon a terrain that the reader will need to examine much more closely on his or her own through careful perusal and self-study.

At least two guides to the social planning literature are available to us. John Friedmann and Barclay Hudson have provided a superb review of theories of the planning process.[1] Their exposition traces the development of major traditions in planning theory from the 1930s to the present. They indicate that there have been four major directions taken by planning theory over this period: philosophical synthesis, rationalism, organizational development, and empiricism. *Philosophical syntheses* are those guiding statements that have charted the broad directions for social planning. These essays range from such arguments as Lindblom's advocacy of "disjointed incrementalism" and his pessimistic view of social planning,[2] on the one hand, to Friedmann's utopian call for "transactive planning," on the other.[3] Etzioni's recommendations for social planning to provide societal guidance represent another philosophical statement in the optimistic genre.[4]

The rationalism or systems theory tradition in planning has been concerned with principles of rational decision making that might be applied to social planning problems. *Rationalism* is Friedmann

[1] John Friedmann and Barclay Hudson, "Knowledge and Action: A Guide to Planning Theory," *Journal of the American Institute of Planners,* 40 (January 1974), 2–16.

[2] Charles Lindblom, *The Intelligence of Democracy: Decision-Making through Mutual Adjustment* (New York: Free Press, 1965).

[3] John Friedmann, *Retracking America* (Garden City, N.Y.: Anchor Books/ Doubleday, 1973).

[4] Amitai Etzioni, *The Active Society* (New York: Free Press, 1968); also see Etzioni and Sarajane Heidt, "Societal Guidance: Toward a Theory of Social Problems," in Erwin O. Smigel, ed., *Handbook on the Study of Social Problems* (Chicago: Rand McNally, 1971), pp. 59–82.

and Hudson's term for lay and conventional notions of the planning process, in which professional, informed decision makers go about making technical decisions, with little input or opinion from the man on the street—for example, when zoning decisions are rendered by professional planning staff members. Friedmann is unenthusiastic about this technocratic form of planning, arguing instead that planning ought to involve widespread citizen participation.[5]

The third tradition discussed by Friedmann and Hudson, *organizational development,* has drawn upon various social science studies of social organizations in order to uncover principles of organizational change that might be utilized in the planning process. Finally, *empiricism* is their label for a number of research inquiries that have been conducted of social planning, either on a national scale such as the Tennessee Valley Authority, or investigations of the outcome of urban planning endeavors. These research findings have, in turn, been incorporated into some of the philosophical dialogues on planning. A major conclusion from the Friedmann and Hudson discussion is that there is no single theoretical structure upon which planners operate, and therefore ". . . planning cannot presently claim to be sustained by a coherent body of theoretical principles." [6]

Richard Bolan has presented another mapping of the planning theory terrain centered on current versions of planning viewpoints.[7] He argues that we can make sense of the myriad viewpoints on planning processes and activities if we conceptualize planning as both (a) a *thinking* process devoted to calculations about the future and (b) a *social* process. Regarding the latter, he points out that thinking about the future is conditioned by ideological influences and social values that mirror the social and cultural environment in which planning takes place. Also, planning is a social process in that successful planning and implementation ultimately rest upon social communication, cooperative relationships among actors in the planning arena, and kindred social factors.

Bolan has developed a diagram consisting of a twelve-celled matrix of the planning terrain based on these thought and social process dimensions, in which thinking or cognitive patterns are

---

[5] Friedmann, *Retracking America.*

[6] Friedmann and Hudson, "Knowledge and Action," p. 13.

[7] Richard S. Bolan, "Mapping the Planning Theory Terrain," in David R. Godschalk, ed., *Planning in America: Learning from Turbulence* (Washington, D.C.: American Institute of Planners, 1974), pp. 13–34. See this entire volume for an assessment of the current state of social planning in America.

further divided into ways of understanding the past and present, ways of imagining the future, and ways of achieving the future. Similarly, four social process contexts or levels of social relations are identified: objective and subjective reality, cultural norms and values, the social institutional framework within which planning occurs, and psychological and individual responses to the social environment.

Bolan's explication of planning perspectives deserves a close reading by anyone who is interested in the state of planning theory. His discussion is too rich and detailed to be captured in a brief paragraph or two. However, some major conclusions from his essay might be noted. First, his comments parallel those of Friedmann and Hudson in indicating that there is no single body of planning theory that the criminal justice planner can rummage through in the search for useful insights. Second, Bolan notes that our substantive knowledge of the past and present is incomplete. The scientific disciplines have not yet delivered all the factual knowledge that we need for effective planning, at the same time that "our ability to plan and intervene effectively in social life is highly dependent on the depth of our understanding." [8] That comment would have a familiar ring to all those who have commented upon the gaps and inadequacies of the criminological research literature which frustrate planning efforts. Bolan also offers the following pithy conclusion about futuristic planning for changes in the social institutions of modern society: "However, substantive imagining of the future of institutional development tends to focus less on significant changes in institutional structure and more on modest adjustments to the existing social order." [9] That observation applies with full force to efforts to think innovatively about alterations in American society that would bring about a significant reduction of lawbreaking.

PUBLIC POLICY, PLANNING, AND POLICY ANALYSIS

In conventional thinking, policymaking and planning are two distinct activities. Policymakers identify broad goals toward which societies, governmental units, or organizations should strive, while planners

---

[8] Ibid., p. 21.

[9] Ibid., p. 24.

are concerned with devising steps for achieving policy ends. In short, policymakers tell us where we ought to go, while planners tell us how to get there.

However, conventional thinking regarding policy formation and planning is misleading, for it is often difficult in practice to distinguish one from the other. On the national level, the president and the Congress are responsible for carving out only the broader outlines of public policy and leave much room for policy formulation to those who man the governmental structure. As a result, it is often difficult to separate the policymaking actions of governmental planners and bureaucrats from their planning activities. In the area of criminal justice, broad policy directives are often outlined by the governor or other state officials, rather than by justice planners. Planners in state planning agencies or at the local level, however, often do go about articulating more specific policies at the same time that they endeavor to discharge the broad mandate given them by the agency administrator, along with public or elected officials. Also, justice planners participate in policymaking when they provide baseline data and analyses of policy alternatives to those above them who are ultimately responsible for charting the course of governmental affairs. Finally, many planning theorists would argue that planning processes and products ought to feed into and inform policymaking activities so that policymaking can result in rational and effective solutions to problems.

It is for reasons of this kind that most of those commentaries on the elements of criminal justice planning that have appeared to date have included policy formation activities as a part of the planning task. For example, Frank and Faust devote most of their attention to policy planning on the part of planners,[10] while Nanus identifies policy planning as one of five types of criminal justice planning.[11]

This same blurring of the distinction between policy formation and planning characterizes the literature on social planning.[12] There

---

[10] James E. Frank and Frederic L. Faust, "A Conceptual Framework for Criminal Justice Planning," *Criminology*, 13 (August 1975), 271–96.

[11] Burt Nanus, "A General Model for Criminal Justice Planning," *Journal of Criminal Justice*, 2 (Winter 1974), 345–56. For a good discussion of some of the problems involved in policy formulation in criminal justice, see Michael Musheno, Dennis Palumbo, and James Levine, "Evaluating Alternatives in Criminal Justice: A Policy-Impact Model," *Crime and Delinquency*, 22 (July 1976), 265–83.

[12] For example, Friedmann and Hudson, "Knowledge and Action."

is an identifiable and rapidly growing field of inquiry that is usually termed "policy analysis" devoted to the study of policy formation and the social influences that account for different policy directions. One can point to a body of literature that constitutes policy analysis theory and research.[13] However, as the Friedmann and Hudson review indicates, planning theorists draw heavily upon this same literature and often include it in their conceptual catalogs without identifying it as separate from planning theory.

We follow the lead of other planning thinkers in this book, by broadening the definition of justice planning to include policy analysis and policy formation as components of the planner role. Neophyte planners would also be well advised to become conversant with the policy analysis literature in their search for useful planning theory.

---

[13] For some useful discussions of policy analysis, see Duncan MacRae, Jr., "Policy Analysis as an Applied Social Science Discipline," *Administration and Society*, 6 (February 1975), 363–88; Stephen L. Elkin, "Political Science and the Analysis of Public Policy," *Public Policy*, 22 (Summer 1974), 399–422; and Robert A. Scott and Arnold Shore, "Sociology and Policy Analysis," *The American Sociologist*, 9 (May 1974), 51–59.

One piece of policy research in criminal justice that the planner ought to examine is Yong Hyo Cho, *Public Policy and Urban Crime* (Cambridge, Mass.: Ballinger, 1974). In this study, Cho examines relationships between crime levels as measured by official statistics, and various police and social service policies in the forty-nine largest U.S. cities and in the forty largest cities in Ohio. Police policy variables have to do with such things as the level of public expenditures for police services, while social service policies involve such matters as federal expenditures on Head Start programs in the individual cities, federal funding of Office of Economic Opportunity programs, public school expenditures, low-rent public-housing availability, and kindred variables. Cho reports that (pp. 193–94): "In general, those social service policies expected to enhance the future opportunities for the disadvantaged tend to show a negative impact on various crimes and those policies instrumental for the improvement of the environmental quality of life tend to show a positive impact on crime." In other words, the more money that is spent on Head Start, employment programs, etc., the higher the crime rates, while large expenditures for public schools, low-rent public housing, and so on, are associated with lower levels of crime. Also, Cho failed to find significant relationships between variations in police policies and crime rates in these cities. One caution here is that statistical associations between large expenditures for employment programs and the like and high crime rates do not mean that the former somehow cause the latter. Instead, these relationships probably indicate that the social and economic conditions that produce crime, and that have led to large expenditures on opportunity-creating programs, are so severe as to be little affected by the social intervention efforts that have been made to date.

PLANNING MODELS AND PLANNING
PROCESSES IN CRIMINAL JUSTICE

The traditional model of the planning enterprise that has been held by many laymen and by some professionals as well is one involving a simple step-by-step process beginning with problem assessment, followed by goal formulation, development of a specific plan that responds to the problem as initially defined, and, finally, solution of the problem. But, at the very least, in the real world the planning process more closely resembles the description offered by Blumstein.[14] He has enumerated seven steps in the planning process: (1) describe the current system; (2) project the future environment; (3) develop alternatives among which to choose; (4) analyze the impact of the alternatives ("pre-evaluation"); (5) allocate resources to the choices and implement them; (6) evaluate the impact ("post-evaluation"); and (7) repeat the process on a regular and continuing basis. The reader will note the similarity of this model to Bolan's characterization of the elements of the thinking process in planning.[15] We emphasize Blumstein's last step, namely, the feedback-loop nature of planning, in which planning is seen as a continuing process that derives guidance from preceding experiences in planning.

As most planners have learned from experience, a planning model is a broad prescription of steps to be taken that become extremely complex in the actual doing. On this point, Alfred Kahn has shed some light on the complexity of the process by describing the elaborate intertwining of planning and action.[16] His summary of the planning process in Figure 6 does not capture all of the richness of his analysis, but it does portray the processual nature and interrelatedness of the various activities associated with social planning.

In Kahn's view, the heart of the planning process is the "definition of the planning task" (Bolan's "understanding of the past and

---

[14] Alfred Blumstein, "A Model to Aid in Planning for the Total Criminal Justice System," in Leonard Oberlander, ed., *Quantitative Tools for Criminal Justice Planning* (Washington, D.C.: Law Enforcement Assistance Administration, 1975), p. 130.

[15] Bolan, "Mapping the Planning Theory Terrain."

[16] Alfred J. Kahn, *Theory and Practice of Social Planning* (New York: Russell Sage, 1969).

FIGURE 6.   Theory and Practice of Social Planning

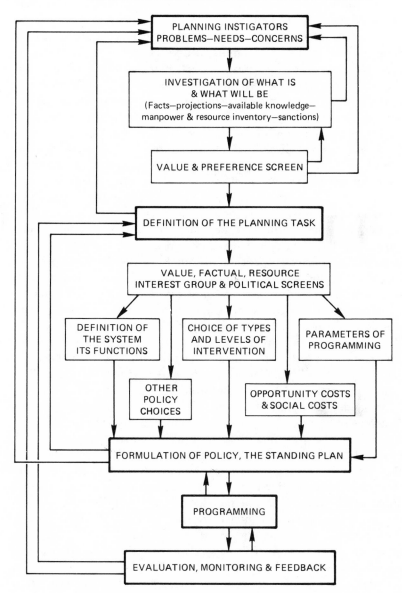

INTERLOCKING CIRCLES AND SPIRALS: PLANNING IN ACTION

PLANNING INSTIGATORS
PROBLEMS—NEEDS—CONCERNS

INVESTIGATION OF WHAT IS
& WHAT WILL BE
(Facts—projections—available knowledge—
manpower & resource inventory—sanctions)

VALUE & PREFERENCE SCREEN

DEFINITION OF THE PLANNING TASK

VALUE, FACTUAL, RESOURCE
INTEREST GROUP & POLITICAL SCREENS

DEFINITION OF
THE SYSTEM
ITS FUNCTIONS

CHOICE OF TYPES
AND LEVELS OF
INTERVENTION

PARAMETERS OF
PROGRAMMING

OTHER
POLICY
CHOICES

OPPORTUNITY COSTS
& SOCIAL COSTS

FORMULATION OF POLICY, THE STANDING PLAN

PROGRAMMING

EVALUATION, MONITORING & FEEDBACK

Source: Kahn, *Theory and Practice of Social Planning*, p. 62.

present"). This definition must be arrived at through a careful assessment of the relevant aspects of social reality and the preferences of the community. According to Kahn, the task definition emerges from these two dimensions of reality.

Let us offer some concrete examples of task definition in the criminal justice area. The example of diversion of juvenile status offenders from the justice system in a particular jurisdiction is a timely and realistic one. In this instance, the planning task definition will evolve from an assessment of such specific social realities as (1) the recent shift in philosophy that calls for limitations upon juvenile court jurisdiction and for "radical nonintervention"; [17] (2) supportive sociological and psychological theories regarding the negative labeling effects of the juvenile court upon status offenders (and other juveniles); and (3) the pressing problem of case overloads in the juvenile courts. Probing of the preferences of the "relevant community" might find that (1) criminal justice agencies and their representatives are not in agreement on whether all, some, or none of the status offenders should be diverted; and (2) existing diversion programs, primarily nonjudicial public and private agencies, do not have sufficient resources or manpower to handle large numbers of youths diverted from juvenile courts. The more specific tasks of investigation of relevant research on existing diversion programs, data and information gathering on the dimensions of the local delinquency problem, resource alternatives, and legal implications are also included in the assessment of social reality and community preferences. What will ultimately emerge as the "planning task" will be a projection or goal statement of the ends to be pursued in the subsequent steps of the planning process—in this case, expanded diversion of youths through the introduction of innovative youth programs into the local juvenile justice structure.

Once the planning tasks or goal statements are articulated, they may lead immediately to formulation of a policy, such as pursuit of legislation to expunge the category of status offenses from statutes and/or expansion of diversion resources to accommodate a projected number of referrals. In all likelihood, however, planning tasks such as diversion will not lend themselves to such straightforward solutions. Kahn's planning scenario suggests that there often are a significant number of considerations to be addressed, including identification of agencies that will provide services and obtaining agreements from them, development of consistent criteria among the agencies, fiscal

---

[17] Edwin M. Schur, *Radical Non-Intervention: Rethinking the Delinquency Problem* (Englewood Cliffs, N.J.: Prentice-Hall, 1973).

projections, and so forth. He also refers to "opportunity and social costs" as considerations interposed between the definition of the planning task and agreement on policy. To illustrate, applied to the diversion issue, this consideration would raise the question of whether diversion will cost more than conventional processing of juveniles or whether it will actually "widen the nets" and bring more children into the official juvenile justice system, creating an expanded problem with new dimensions. That is, diversion might end up providing services for many children who would have remained outside the juvenile justice system had diversion not been developed. Clearly, these are weighty considerations that may compel planners to go "back to the planning drawing board" to rethink some of their original plans.

Obviously, application of the planning process as outlined by Kahn to the diversion issue is much more complex than described here. However, his model graphically portrays the steps and phases involved in planning as inevitably processual and interactive, rather than being an orderly road map that takes the traveler to point B from point A without detour. Planning moves down a road filled with many switchbacks, detours, and even dead ends, which must be traveled with full anticipation that retracing and retracking will be part of the process. Parenthetically, the issue of how best to deal with juvenile status offenders is not unlike many other criminal justice problems which too often are thought of as simple community, agency, or legal matters and only too infrequently as complex planning challenges.

We probably do not need to offer many more examples to emphasize this point regarding planning as a *feedback process*. But consider another case. Suppose that a state corrections agency assesses the needs of incarcerated offenders (definition of the planning task) and concludes that work release centers are needed throughout the state. In all likelihood, it will be no easy task to establish that network of centers. The correctional authorities will face a good deal of hostility in the state legislature, as well as in the local sites chosen for work release units. In the course of implementing this general policy of graduated release, many of the initial decisions will have to be modified in the light of community responses and other unanticipated results of the initial planning and policy definition steps. Or, finally, suppose that the administrative officials of a county decide to convert the county sheriff's department from a paramilitary organization to an organization structured around team policing. Much effort would have to go into the initial task definition, involving assessment of crime patterns, community attitudes about police reorganization, departmental receptivity to reorganization, and so on. A considerable period of experimentation with new policing patterns, monitoring of these efforts, and further planning would also be required, in order to iron out the wrinkles in this new organizational fabric.

It must be apparent that we agree with a number of other writers who have argued that monitoring and evaluation are important contributory activities in the planning process. We shall deal with the matter of program evaluation techniques in some detail in Chapter 7.

PLANNING FORMS AND SYSTEM CHANGE

Many criminal justice planners and those agency and public representatives involved in the criminal justice planning arena may not accept the apocalyptic visions of futurists who predict disaster for our society if we continue to rely upon our present institutional arrangements that are unresponsive to today's social ills. Few would disagree, however, that change of some degree is imperative and that new approaches to crime control or reduction are in order, with opinions on this matter ranging from advocacy of simple improvements in the efficiency of existing criminal justice machinery to massive overhaul of the justice system, along with large-scale alterations in the social-economic structure of society. In a planning framework, this range of conflicting viewpoints can be managed more constructively by the planner when proposed objectives are visually displayed, discussed, and weighed in terms of their change potential. The conceptual scheme that follows is one method of identifying specific planning objectives in a hierarchical perspective that also identifies the degree of change anticipated through adoption of the objective.

We have already introduced the language of tactical and strategic planning in Chapter 4, in our summary of the views of Daniel Glaser.[18] Planners in a number of fields frequently use the "strategic" and "tactical" terms when referring to particular planning approaches. *Strategic planning* ordinarily refers to long-range and comprehensive planning set within a time frame of four or five years, while *tactical planning* involves short-term and more narrowly fo-

---

[18] Daniel Glaser, *Strategic Criminal Justice Planning* (Rockville, Md.: National Institute of Mental Health, 1975).

cused planning carried on over a period of a few weeks, a few months, or an annual or biennial budget cycle. The terms *ad hoc planning* or *opportunistic planning* are also encountered as substitute terms for *tactical planning*.

Friedmann's Approach

We prefer to utilize Friedmann's notions of "allocative" and "innovative" planning.[19] Glaser considers the terms "allocative" and "innovative" as roughly comparable to "tactical" and "strategic," but we think that Friedmann's terminology provides for more precise analysis. We employ a number of Friedmann's concepts in the following paragraphs, although we have made some significant modifications in them.

Friedmann associates allocative planning with "functional rationality" as manifested in the well-known Planning-Programming-Budgeting System (PPBS), that is, the allocation of existing resources to achieve stated objectives. While allocative planning may be fairly comprehensive in scope, it is nontheless focused essentially on system maintenance and a continuation of the balance of forces and influences that guide current organizational activities. The planning efforts that have emerged at state and local levels under LEAA have been primarily allocative in character. The planning focus has been "problem" oriented and has resulted in projects that have stressed reduction of problem phenomena such as recidivism among parolees or increasing burglary arrests, but only rarely has planning addressed the underlying causes of specific crime phenomena. For example, the project objectives in the majority of LEAA-funded programs have emphasized allocation of resources (money, manpower, etc.) to do something about what Friedmann refers to as "collective phenomena" or the *symptoms* of the crime problem, but only rarely has criminal justice planning challenged the fundamental institutional arrangements or activities that available knowledge indicates have some relationship to crime and delinquency causation, and only rarely has justice planning led to advocacy of improved methods for dealing with these phenomena. For example, little has been attempted in the way of overhauling the public school system in order to alleviate the frustrations it creates for many youngsters, little has been done to

---

[19] Friedmann, *Retracking America.*

open up employment opportunities for juveniles, little has been accomplished in the way of regeneration of urban neighborhoods, and little has been attempted regarding other sources of criminality identified by the President's Commission on Law Enforcement and Administration of Justice.[20]

Innovative planning, on the other hand, is oriented toward action and the mobilization of resources to effect institutional change. Innovative planning proceeds on the assumption that the institutional arrangements—that is, the "guidance systems" that presently constitute our societal structure—are functioning inadequately, thus leading to the problems we face. Friedmann presents a listing of components of the guidance systems, which comprises four categories: political and legal, economic and financial, administrative, and cognitive and planning.[21]

Friedmann cites crime in the streets as a "collective phenomenon" which is an outgrowth of the present guidance system in America.[22] It is an outcome that results from the intricate intertwining of social, economic, political, statutory, administrative, and planning arrangements that exist in American society today. He contends that until we move from incremental or allocative planning to innovative planning we will continue to attack the crime problem in a relatively superficial manner, applying "band-aid solutions" and affecting minimally the elements of the guidance system that contribute to the crime phenomenon. He asserts:

> If crime in the streets is a collective phenomenon (as revealed in the statistics of the FBI), adding policemen to the force may reverse the trend in a particular district, but the system of guidance institutions will continue to generate a certain *rate* of criminal behavior, and criminal actions will simply be displaced to other parts of the city."[23]

---

[20] The President's Commission on Law Enforcement and Administration of Justice, *The Challenge of Crime in a Free Society* (Washington, D.C.: Government Printing Office, 1967).

[21] Friedmann, *Retracking America*, p. 145.

[22] Ibid., p. 144.

[23] Ibid., p. 144. This claim is quite plausible, but it may be too facile. Reppetto has presented an equally plausible line of argument regarding the displacement of crime. He suggests that some kinds of crime, particularly property offenses, may be reduced through such measures as increased police patrol in a particular

There is an important point to be made about this notion of guidance systems, namely, that these underlying structural arrangements that produce various "collective phenomena," including crime, are not all of the same order or pervasiveness. Some of the political or administrative arrangements that are implicated in certain patterns of lawbreaking may be relatively identifiable and amenable to alteration through planning and action. At the same time, other guidance system variables, particularly those revolving around economic inequities and economic precariousness in American society, may be much more complex and markedly more difficult to attack. A planner would find the task of restructuring the correctional component of a state criminal justice system to be a markedly easier assignment than one of considering ways in which economic strains within a state might be modified.

Much of Friedmann's commentary on planning centers on societal guidance system elements of the most complex kind. The planning task he discusses seems more centrally concerned with improving the general quality of life in American society than it is with more modest efforts at restructuring some of the specific institutional arrangements that contribute to particular social problems. In the case of crime, for example, it is likely that he would be more concerned with such things as massive changes in income distribution in the United States in order to alleviate economic precariousness as a "root cause" of crime than he would be with more immediate planning efforts, such as restructuring of particular school systems and opening up more employment opportunities for parolees or youths in a local community.

We have no quarrel with the thesis that the "root causes" of lawbreaking ought to be addressed if we hope to make drastic reductions in the crime problem. At the same time, we hasten to add that it is markedly easier to talk about "root causes" than it is to identify them and indicate steps that can be taken to attack them. The large-scale social and economic reforms that are hinted at here are not the stuff of current criminal justice planning. Justice planners do not

---

district. He argues that impulses to steal may sometimes be markedly influenced by opportunities to steal, so that if opportunities are reduced, motivation to engage in theft may decline. Also, he contends that even if potential offenders continue to be motivated to engage in crime, they may find it difficult to go to another part of the community in order to engage in lawbreaking. For example, garden-variety offenders do not always have adequate means of transportation at their disposal. See Thomas A. Reppetto, "Crime Prevention and the Displacement Phenomenon," *Crime and Delinquency*, 22 (April 1976), 166–77.

have the major responsibility for policy choices and decisions of that magnitude. Instead, their tasks have much more to do with specific modifications in particular institutional arrangements.

It is for reasons of this kind that we restrict the term *innovative planning* to relatively focused planning problems normally encountered in the ongoing criminal justice system. We have conjured up another, somewhat inelegant, term, *macro planning*, to refer to those larger societal change endeavors of particular concern to Friedmann.

The Tasks of Innovative Planning

So much for Friedmann's basic concepts and our modifications of them. Let us now examine his outline of the "innovative planning task." Here he emphasizes a break with the traditional planning model that is followed in allocative planning and calls for a performance analysis of the organizational characteristics of the guidance system relative to a given problem or collective phenomenon. Such an effort involves a series of interrelated steps:

1. Identify and describe the problem situation as a collective phenomenon.

2. Identify and analyze the relevant forms and patterns of collective behavior.

3. Identify the institutions of the guidance system that are thought to be primarily responsible for this behavior.

4. Analyze the specific performance characteristics of these institutions as they relate to the collective behavior identified in (2) above in terms of their degree of autonomy, responsiveness, innovativeness, effectiveness, efficiency, and legitimacy.

5. Relate these performance characteristics to particular organizational features of the guidance system, such as hierarchy, centralization, participation, information processing, and organizational linkages.

6. On the basis of this analysis, formulate specific proposals for structural innovation in the guidance system that are expected, if carried out, to change the relevant performance, produce a different outcome in terms of collective behavior,

and result in significant improvements in the initial problem situation; and propose a strategy for innovative action.

7. Take part in the realization of this strategy, making the adjustments that are necessary in the course of the action.[24]

When this planning approach is used in analyzing a particular phenomenon, it alerts the planner to a recognition of some of the basic but relatively hidden dimensions of the problem, as well as to an understanding of the elements of the guidance system that perpetuate it. Applied to a particular problem area in the criminal justice field, the planner can begin to formulate multidimensional solutions at both the service delivery and structural levels.

A Planning Continuum

Using Friedmann's basic vocabulary as a starting point, as well as his outline of the planning task, we can visualize the planning process as a continuum with "allocative planning" at one end of the scale and "macro planning" at the other. This continuum highlights the range of planning objectives, beginning with program maintenance, to alterations in program structure, and, finally, to alterations in societal structure. This continuum includes another category, "re-allocative planning," as well as "innovative planning." *Re-allocative planning* refers to activities that are focused on an intermediate level of change between allocative and innovative endeavors. This term emphasizes the fact that certain planning goals or objectives involve hoped-for results that focus at least to some degree both on program performance or impact and on certain institutional arrangements related to service delivery, but these goals or objectives are not as extensive or broad as is implied in the term *innovative*.

This conceptual scheme also distinguishes between (a) objectives that are focused on the structural arrangements of particular delivery systems such as police agencies or courts and (b) objectives that are focused both on structural change *and* on improving the impact of the system. For example, a planning objective might focus on reducing burglary rates, producing fewer negotiated pleas of guilty, or delivering more group counseling to incarcerated offenders; or it

---

24 Ibid., p. 164.

might focus more heavily on utilizing police manpower more efficiently while maintaining crime rates at current levels, reorganizing the work patterns in the court, or restructuring the treatment activities within training school cottages so as to implicate both cottage parents and social workers in them. This model is shown in Figure 7 and is further elaborated in the following planning examples. We offer three examples in each category (except macro planning): one from the police component, one from the judicial area, and one dealing with corrections. Some macro-level endeavors are noted elsewhere in the remainder of this chapter.

Allocative Planning: One of the basic forms of planning concerned with actions that affect distribution of limited resources among competing groups or users.

> *A-1 Gradation:*   A planned objective that will leave unchanged the basic structure of the program delivery system and simply maintain the level of service.

>> *Example I:*   Replacement of sworn police officers by civilians in non–law enforcement roles (i.e., clerks, dispatchers), while a desirable objective, probably would not in itself affect either the organizational structure or the service delivery provided by the police agency.

>> *Example II:*   Employment of paraprofessionals in the public defender's office, to be assigned to interviewing indigent clients in jail, replacing lawyers in that assignment.

>> *Example III:*   Introduction of television monitoring system into a state penitentiary, which reduces the number of correctional officers needed to man the shifts. Subsequent transfer of some guards to employment at other institutions, as vacancies are created through terminations, resignations, retirement, etc.

In these examples of allocative planning at the A-1 level, change of the most modest kind is involved. The program or project objective is simply to *maintain* the police, public defender, or prison

A CONTINUUM OF PLANNING FORMS

MACRO PLANNING OBJECTIVES

Improves performance level and involves major alteration in societal structure.

INNOVATIVE PLANNING OBJECTIVES

I-1

Maintains performance level but involves major alteration in service delivery structure.

I-2

Improves performance level and involves major alteration in service delivery structure.

RE-ALLOCATIVE PLANNING OBJECTIVES

Re-1

Maintains performance level but involves initial alteration of service delivery structure.

Re-2

Improves performance and involves initial alteration of service delivery structure.

ALLOCATIVE PLANNING OBJECTIVES

A-1

Maintains performance level and service delivery structure.

A-2

No change in structure but improves efficiency and/or effectiveness of service delivery.

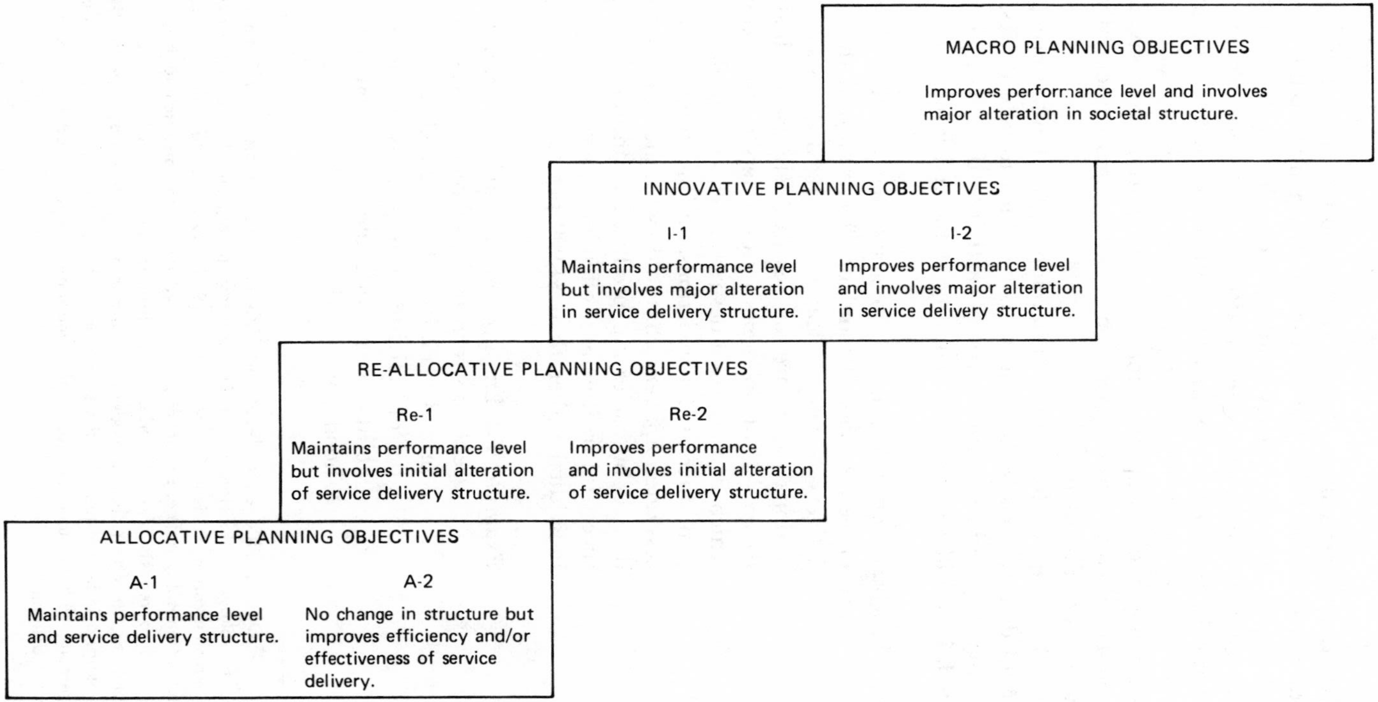

FIGURE 7.   A Continuum of Planning Forms

operations at their current levels. In the police case, service levels would stay the same, the size of the police agency would stay the same, but over time the agency would come to have a larger proportion of civilian employees, due to attrition of sworn officers, who would not be replaced under this plan. In the same way, the public defender's office would remain the same size but would gain an increased number of paraprofessionals, with important cost savings to the county. Finally, prison operations would remain essentially unchanged under this plan.

But suppose that a plan is developed to relieve sworn police officers of desk responsibilities and to assign them to field duties, thus increasing the police agency's patrol activity. If that plan were adopted, it would be a case of planning at the A-2 level.

> *A-2 Gradation:* A planned objective that is intended to improve the efficiency and/or effectiveness of the service delivery system but leaves unchanged the basic organizational structure or service delivery method. *Effectiveness* of an organization refers to the extent to which it produces a desired effect, i.e., burglary reduction, increased convictions, or increased parole success rates. *Efficiency* has to do with the extent to which desired outcomes are produced at minimal cost, i.e., successful treatment of offenders at a cost of $2,000 per individual rather than $4,000 per case.

> *Example I:* Employment of civilian employees to replace sworn police officers on desk jobs will provide additional personnel to assign to patrol activities, thus increasing the agency's ability to provide more complete neighborhood coverage.[25]

---

[25] One real-life example of this kind has been reported by Skogan. See Wesley G. Skogan, "Efficiency and Effectiveness in Big-City Police Departments," *Public Administration Review*, 36 (May–June 1976), 278–86. He indicates that the St. Paul, Minnesota, police began a policy in 1970 of not dispatching patrol cars in response to reports of theft under $100. Instead, reporting citizens were sent a questionnaire on which they provided the information needed by investigative officers. Skogan indicates that the theft clearance rate remained the same under this arrangement, with presumably more police manpower being freed for other law enforcement assignments.

Example II: Employment of law school students to work as investigative aids in the county prosecutor's office, allowing more deputy prosecutors to concentrate upon prosecutorial work, thereby reducing the time lag between arrest and prosecution of persons charged.

Example III: Employment of additional psychiatric social workers within a correctional medical facility who are assigned to provide more intensive counseling to incarcerated sex offenders.

Re-Allocative Planning: A form of planning focused on maintaining or improving service delivery through initial alterations in the service delivery structure.

Re-1 Gradation: A planned objective that maintains the service level but involves an initial alteration of the service delivery structure.

Example I: Police officers in community X discontinue arresting Skid Road drunks and lodging them in city jail. The city administration announces a policy of taking Skid Road drunks to city-financed detoxification centers, which are to be operated as part of the municipal court–city jail system.

The reader ought to consult Skogan's article for other commentary on police functioning as well. Skogan discusses *police efficiency* and *police effectiveness.* Police effectiveness is usually measured by the extent to which crimes reported to the police are cleared by arrest, hence a relatively effective department would be one that produced arrests in 50 percent of the reported cases, rather than in only 25 percent or 10 percent. Police efficiency is more complex, for it involves calculations of police effectiveness divided by police expenditures. In other words, department A would be said to be more efficient than department B if both had the same crime clearance rates, but with comparatively lower manpower costs in department A.

In an analysis of 1970 data on cities having over 50,000 population, Skogan reports that the findings indicate that the most effective police departments also tend to be the most efficient ones. The efficient departments operate effectively at lower cost through the use of computers and allied technical aids.

Example II: Community X develops a system of youth services bureaus which will provide for the diversion of 30 percent of all referred status offenders from the juvenile court.

Example III: Establishment of "parole teams" on a regional basis within a state, in which different members of the parole teams are assigned to deal with particular parolee groups, such as semiprofessional property offenders, check forgers, or sex offenders. This organizational pattern replaces the customary structure in which individual parole agents handle large and heterogeneous caseloads of parolees.

The objectives indicated in the three examples above would not necessarily produce marked improvement in the performance level of the police, juvenile court, or parole agency. However, structural changes of the sort suggested here would presumably be intended to produce some improvement in the impact of these operations, so that the difference between this planned change and category Re-2 should be viewed as a matter of degree.

Re-2 Gradation: A planned objective that is intended to improve the performance level and also involves an initial alteration of the service delivery structure.

Example I: Community Y develops team policing, in which generalist and specialist police roles (patrolman vs. detective) are combined in decentralized patrol/investigative teams within a specific geographical area in which they function. It is anticipated that the teams will be more effective than the existing patrol/investigative organizational arrangement, in terms of crime reduction. In addition, closer working relationships between police teams and community members are predicted from this organizational change, as well as increased departmental morale.

Example II: Development of a special rape investigation program, a rape-reporting "hotline," and a specialized rape-counseling program for rape victims within the prosecutor's office. The rape investigation deputies provide intensified investigation of reported rape incidents, while the "hotline" encourages increased reporting of rapes. The rape-counseling structure is designed not only to encourage rape victims to testify fully in court but, and more important, to markedly reduce much of the trauma for rape victims that has commonly been encountered in the past.

Example III: Development of specialized probation units in a particular state, in which regular probation officers, special employment-education counselors, and paraprofessionals are brought together to form probation teams, operating out of urban centers that also include temporary living space for some probationers. Sentenced offenders who would normally be sent to prison are assigned instead to these specialized probation units, on the assumption that the coordinated and specialized intensive supervision and assistance they receive will increase their prospects for successful postconviction adjustments.

In these examples of planning at the Re-2 level, alterations in organizational structure are intended to achieve significant improvement in the performance of the organization. At the same time, these alterations would not drastically change the service delivery system. The planning objective itself might have evolved from a step-by-step assessment of the problems associated with traditional police, court, or correctional operations, but for political or administrative reasons only a beginning alteration in the structure was considered possible. The primary reason for our introduction of the term *re-allocative* is highlighted by these examples. An intermediate level of planned change, falling somewhere between allocative and innovative planning, may be most feasible even though the initial assessment or diagnosis of the linkage of collective phenomena to elements of the guidance system may call for innovative planning.

Innovative Planning: One of the basic forms of planning concerned with actions that produce significant changes in social institution patterns.

> *I-1 Gradation:*   A planned objective that maintains the performance level but prescribes a major alteration in social institution patterns.

>> *Example I:*   All twenty-five separate police agencies in a particular metropolitan area merge into a single metropolitan police agency, administered by one command structure, and integrated into a single police unit in all other ways as well.

>> *Example II:*   In cooperation with the juvenile court and police agencies, community Z establishes a program providing for the diversion of *all* status offenders from the police and juvenile justice system, with some diverted offenders being sent to youth service–youth advocacy agencies and others being released outright without receiving services of any kind.

>> *Example III:*   Following the Massachusetts example, state X closes all of its ten training schools for juveniles and establishes a statewide network of youth outpatient treatment centers and other programs for juveniles. Additionally, sizable numbers of youths are released to private agencies.

As in the two categories of re-allocative planning, some degree of improvement in program impact, as indexed by reductions in crime rates, increased rehabilitation of court wards, or improved parole behavior through deinstitutionalization, would probably be anticipated from these instances of innovative planning. But reorganization of metropolitan police might be undertaken because of financial savings to the local governments concerned.[26] Similarly, diversion of status

---

[26] This matter of police consolidation is complex. Ostrom and Parks have conducted research on a number of police departments which indicates that those departments that spend the largest sums per capita and which engage in various inno-

offenders might be advocated with the hope that only a relatively modest improvement in program impact upon wards retained within the court would result. Also, the expectation might be that deinstitutionalization would save the state money even though it might not produce marked changes in delinquency rates statewide.

I-2 Gradation: A planned objective that is intended to improve the performance level and which also involves a major alteration in social institution patterns.

Example I: All twenty-five separate police agencies in a particular metropolitan area merge into a single metropolitan policy agency, administered by one command structure. Team policing is adopted through the new metropolitan police department, replacing the traditional paramilitary organizational structure. Computer technology is widely utilized, along with extensive research activities designed to improve police response to crime, aid in the detection of crime, etc.

Example II: State *A* creates a new juvenile justice code which removes status offenses from the jurisdiction of the juvenile court but also provides state financial support for a series of state guidance clinics to which parents and children can go for family counseling. The legislation also severely curtails the jurisdiction of juvenile courts and limits them to handling of "serious delinquents," which is a category that is specifically and narrowly defined in the statute. In addition, a new state

---

vative training policies and the like are viewed most negatively by citizens. In communities where departments of that kind are located, citizens are more likely to think that crime is increasing, that the police respond more slowly to citizen complaints, and that the police are more dishonest. See Elinor Ostrom and Roger B. Parks, "Suburban Police Departments: Too Many, Too Small?" *Urban Affairs Annual Review* (Beverly Hills, Calif.: Sage Publications, 1974), VII, 367–402. Ostrom and Parks suggest that these variations in police structure are linked to city and department size; thus police agencies in the largest cities spend more money per capita on policing and utilize innovative police techniques.

youth agency is created, charged with the responsibility for guiding local schools to modify their programs in order to make school more attractive and rewarding to youths. This state agency also has the responsibility for creating increased employment opportunities for out-of-school youths and is charged with the general responsibility for developing preventive programs across the entire state.

Example III: As a result of a long-range planning effort within a state, legislation is enacted which expunges a number of offenses from the statute books, so that certain forms of behavior become "decriminalized." At the same time, legislation decriminalizing drunkenness is passed, but the courts are empowered to carry out civil commitment of alcoholics to detoxification centers which are established throughout the state. State funding is provided for these detoxification centers, so that they have a number of resources available to them in attempting to reestablish treated alcoholics in stable life patterns.

This same long-range planning produces a number of major changes in the correctional system within the state. Specialized probation units similar to those described in Re-2 are created, as are parallel parole units. County probation departments throughout the state are encouraged to place large numbers of persons in these special probation units, rather than send them to prison. A state-funded "subvention" program is created, through which counties receive state funds to subsidize their probation services, with the level of funding being commensurate with the reductions in prison commitments they produce.[27]

---

[27] The planner might study rather closely Paul Lerman's report on the probation subsidy program that was conducted in California. See Lerman, *Community Treatment and Social Control* (Chicago: University of Chicago Press, 1975). His anal-

The long-range planning also involves development of sentencing and paroling guidelines, in which incarcerated offenders are kept in prison for only short periods of time in most cases (six months to one year). Also, steps are taken to establish state programs of expanding employment opportunities for ex-offenders, and expanded educational opportunities through providing state education loans to ex-offenders, and a number of other actions are taken to "open up legitimate opportunities" for offenders and to provide them with a "stake in conformity."

A few concluding words are in order regarding this scheme of planning forms. We have already noted that some planned changes are centered most heavily on system reorganization and less on improvements in the impact of the service in question, while in other instances an increased program impact is a major goal, but also that this matter of differing emphases is a matter of degree. Nearly all organizational changes are made, in part, in the hope that organizational impact will be heightened to some extent. A second comment is that some of the examples offered above have to do with planned changes in more than one part of the justice system, although they are centered on police agencies, courts, or corrections. Most important, some of the examples we have offered may strike many readers as "unrealistic," which means that they would not be likely to receive an enthusiastic response from the general public at the present time when calls for a return to harsher sentences, restoration of the death penalty, and the like, are being voiced from some quarters. Although we concede that point, we do not believe that these are unrealistic examples in any other way.

---

ysis indicated that although the subsidy program resulted in fewer commitments from the counties to the California Youth Authority, those who were committed received lengthier stays than formerly. Additionally, the number of youths who were incarcerated for short periods of time at the county level *increased* during the subsidy program. Finally, Lerman's investigation indicates that this program did *not* result in savings to the state in operating expenses.

SOME OBSERVATIONS ON MACRO PLANNING

The examples of planning that we have considered in this chapter, and most of the others scattered throughout the preceding pages, such as youth diversion efforts, would be unlikely to bring about massive reductions in lawbreaking in American society. A candid assessment would suggest that about the best that could be hoped for from most of the innovations discussed to this point would be that they might allow us to "keep the lid on" crime, maintaining it under reasonable control and perhaps reducing some of it in some places in the nation. Ideally, the criminal justice system would also provide the basic elements of fairness and humane treatment to those who are processed through that machinery.

Suppose that we were to begin thinking about how marked reductions in total lawbreaking in our society might be achieved. That kind of thinking would involve us in macro planning, in which fundamental alterations in the social order would be required, in order to get at the "root causes" of criminality. In Friedmann's terms, planning directed at the core guidance systems of society would be required.[28]

Two basic directions have been suggested by those who have considered the question of macro change and criminality—movement toward a "garrison state" or major shifts toward some version of state socialism.

The most outspoken advocate of a "garrison state" approach to crime reduction is James Q. Wilson.[29] Wilson explores the argument that criminality is often a response to economic precariousness but rejects that thesis on the grounds that many individuals steal during times of high employment and affluence. Although he acknowledges that crime rates are high among young unemployed persons, at one point he argues that

---

[28] Our views on macrosocial variables and macroplanning parallel those of Etzioni and Heidt. See Amitai Etzioni and Sarajane Heidt, "Societal Guidance: Toward a Theory of Social Problems," in Erwin O. Smigel, ed., *Handbook on the Study of Social Problems* (Chicago: Rand McNally, 1971), pp. 59–82.

[29] James Q. Wilson, *Thinking about Crime* (New York: Basic Books, 1975). For an incisive discussion of the writings of "the new conservatives," including Wilson, see Kirkpatrick Sale, "The New Conservatives: Old Whine in New Bottles," *Mother Jones*, 1 (June 1976), 29–55.

if legitimate opportunities for work are unavailable, many young persons will turn to crime; but if criminal opportunities are profitable, many young persons will not take those legitimate jobs that exist. The benefits of work and the costs of crime must be increased simultaneously; to increase one but not the other makes sense only if one assumes that young people are irrational.[30]

Throughout most of his commentary on the crime problem in American society, Wilson comes down more firmly on the side of increasing the costs of crime to offenders than on increasing the attractiveness of work.

Wilson's "hardheaded pragmatism" is often disguised in graceful language, so that his message appears to be that of an eminently reasonable man. Still, critics of his views would argue that garden-variety property crime commonly arises out of perceptions of "relative deprivation" on the part of offenders, rather than from economic strain per se.[31] Along a related line, Skolnick has scored Wilson for his lack of concern about white-collar crime, abuse of power by public officials, and other forms of lawbreaking additional to garden-variety property crime, along with his ahistorical approach which fails to examine the social and economic roots out of which the contemporary "crime wave" has developed.[32]

In his critique of Wilson's book, Skolnick indicates that it stands in marked contrast to liberal proposals for crime reduction that have been offered frequently in the past:

As an antidote to the crime problem, changes in the social and economic structures of society have been proposed by a variety of students of crime in American society, from staffs of national commissions through scores of independent scholars. Such proposals have, on the whole, been received with little enthusiasm from the

---

[30] Ibid., p. 202.

[31] C. Ronald Chester, "Relative Deprivation as a Cause of Property Crime," *Crime and Delinquency*, 22 (January 1976), 17–30; also see Jackson Toby, "The Prospects for Reducing Delinquency Rates in Industrial Societies," *Federal Probation*, 27 (December 1963), 23–25; and Sheldon Danziger and David Wheeler, "The Economics of Crime: Punishment or Income Redistribution," *Review of Social Economy*, 33 (October 1975), 113–30.

[32] Jerome H. Skolnick, "Are More Jails the Answer?" *Dissent*, 23 (Winter 1976), 95–97.

politically powerful. Nor has the general public been persuaded to try, much less accept, a social structural approach to crime, even though generations of scholars have urged massive social changes in American society as the only humane and democratic response.[33]

Wilson's central message is a pessimistic one that suggests that dramatic reductions in levels of crime are beyond any realistic hope of achievement. He argues that even if it is true that crime is linked to structural inequities in the economic system and other "root causes" of that sort, we can do little about these matters. Accordingly, he would have us build more prisons and keep persons in them for longer periods of time, along with a number of other steps to increase the certainty and severity of punishment.

We are not concerned here with whether Wilson has sound logic and adequate empirical evidence on his side, even though we do agree with those who find flaws in his argument. Instead, our point is that if we were to take Wilson seriously and were to endeavor to create the kind of social world that his recommendations imply, we would surely have to anticipate living in a vastly changed social environment. His proposals call for heroic investments of public funds in the construction of new prisons, a variety of steps in the direction of reducing due-process protections for alleged offenders so as to increase the certainty and swiftness of punishment, and numerous other social control measures that would be likely to exacerbate the hostility between the underdogs in our society and the rest of us. In short, it is wholly unlikely that a bit of tampering here and there with the social structure and the investment of a few billion dollars more in criminal justice system operations will produce the kind of social order hinted at in the pages of Wilson's book. Skolnick has put the matter well:

> Ultimately, there are no simple punitive remedies to the crime problem in a society valuing freedom, democracy, and due process of law. And that is one reason why, in thinking about crime, we must finally understand that it is utopian not to consider its causes. Either we attend to altering the social and economic bases of crime or we grope our way toward a false realism—a garrison state, increasingly controlled by those possessing the force of arms and the keys to the prison.[34]

---

[33] Ibid., p. 95.

[34] Ibid., pp. 97.

The alternative to Wilson's future society is some version of state socialism, by which we mean some kind of social-economic structure involving a markedly increased degree of governmental management of the economy. This alternative society would be one in which significant income redistribution would be effected through governmental action involving such measures as the closing off of existing tax loopholes, major revision of the tax structure, and more regulation of corporate activities and vigorous prosecution of corporate crime. Actions of this kind would be undertaken in order that sustained attacks on urban slums, chronic unemployment, and other conditions could be mounted. These are the kinds of drastic reforms in the societal "guidance systems" that are implied in the report of the President's Commission on Law Enforcement and Administration of Justice, although that report refrained from making explicit recommendations of this kind.[35]

We have already commented on some of the difficulties of macro planning. It is relatively easy to enumerate a number of structural deficiencies that need repair, such as inadequate housing, chronic underemployment, and various other aspects of contemporary society, but it is not so easy to agree upon specific remedies that might be applied to these problems. Even so, these are not matters that are beyond human capacity to consider. For example, the Humphrey-Hawkins Full Employment Bill now being considered by the Congress, which endeavors to reduce unemployment to 3 percent of the adult labor force by 1980, is one relatively modest macro step that would be likely to have a significant impact on lawbreaking. On a more dramatic scale, New Left historian William Appleman Williams has proposed some radical revisions of the entire social and economic structure of the United States.[36] He has argued for the creation of regional communities and a version of regional socialism to replace the present bureaucratic empire represented by the federal government. Under his plan, the economics of regionalism would involve retention of most private property by citizens, but with energy resources, water, and transportation facilities being designated as social property. These would be community owned and would be allocated by citizens through a democratic process. In this new form of regional socialism envisioned by Williams, creation and management of this structure would be

---

[35] President's Commission on Law Enforcement, *Challenge of Crime.*

[36] William Appleman Williams, "Where Are These Politicians Taking Us?" *Northwest Magazine,* August 15, 1976, pp. 10–25; also see Williams, *The Contours of American History* (Chicago: Quadrangle, 1966).

carried on through democratic processes into which the citizenry would make continual contributions. Also, computer technology and other management tools of modern society would be harnessed in the interests of a more rational political economy.

Several points leap to mind regarding Williams's recommendations. First, they parallel the proposals of Friedmann, which urge that renovations and alterations be made in societal guidance systems. Indeed, Williams points to some specific guidance system modifications in his portrayal of regional socialism. Second, Williams's proposals do not speak directly to the question of crime reduction in American society, although they certainly would be expected to have positive consequences in that area. Third, and most important, these recommendations for the establishment of regional socialism have a utopian ring to them, in that they would require restructuring of the economic and political processes on a heroic scale. Even so, these proposals are not palpably wrongheaded or incapable of achievement.

We suggest that it is possible to conjure up realistic visions of a new form of American society in which the quality of life would be markedly improved. There is no shortage of persons who are capable of developing workable models of societal organization toward which the United States might move and which would quite probably experience less crime than is currently the case. But there is little reason to suppose that major steps in the direction of one or another of these alternate futures are going to be occurring within the next few years in this country. In all likelihood such developments will occur, if at all, only after a prolonged and severe period of political, economic, and social dislocation, in which the deficiencies of the present societal structure become apparent to the vast majority of citizens. Finally, as we indicated earlier in this chapter, these social and economic reform proposals take us far beyond the current problems of criminal justice planning into the area of basic national policy. As a result, we must leave any extended discussion of macro-level planning and change to another book.

SUMMARY

Let us pull some of the strands of commentary in Chapters 5 and 6 together into a summary statement. To begin with, we agree with those who have contended that the crime problem and the criminal justice machinery in the United States cry out for much more sophisticated planning activities than have been common in the past. The evidence is all around us, indicating that if new and more effective ways of responding to criminality in this country are not discovered and implemented through planning, the justice system will ultimately collapse under the sheer weight of numbers of new offenders coming into it, along with recidivists returning through the revolving doors of the structure.

We have emphasized that justice planning calls for persons who are as highly trained and informed as the current state of knowledge will allow. These individuals need to be equipped with a detailed understanding of the crime problem, crime patterns, and crime causation. They must be well grounded in the empirical evidence at hand regarding the social organizational workings of elements of the justice system, along with a detailed appreciation of the existing evidence regarding the effectiveness or ineffectiveness of various kinds of treatment and intervention activity. Professional planners must also be well grounded in the political and social realities within which justice planning must be carried out. Finally, justice planners require a body of planning theory and methodology.

We reiterate a point made in Chapter 4 having to do with *system change* rather than *offender change* as the central focus of planning. Although planning endeavors are ultimately designed to improve upon the effectiveness of crime control or intervention efforts, thereby reducing crime rates or recidivism, the major thrust of planning is organizational alterations. "People-changing" activities ought to be engaged in as a result of planning, but they are not themselves examples of planning.

Throughout Chapter 6 we stressed the importance of comprehensive planning—or, in parallel terms, innovative or strategic planning. We hold that planning ought to be considerably more than "projecting." Although the LEAA requirement that states prepare master plans is a reasonable one, we need to be on guard against the fossilization of master plans that has been the experience of city planning. There was a time when planners went about creating grand designs for "the city beautiful," which were taken as immutable models that would govern how the city would unfold. But the actual history of urban growth has been one in which unplanned growth and change have been dominant. Modern-day urban planners tend to look upon comprehensive plans in a different light, for they view them as providing a general guide to urban development at the same time that they anticipate alterations and modifications occurring in the overall plan as the community prospers. The master plan is now treated as a working model that will be modified as the planning *process* continues.

We stressed a similar view of justice planning in this chapter. Master plans and other complex planning outputs are best viewed as guides for the criminal justice system, to be modified, expanded, and altered in the light of new experience, particularly as evidence from program evaluation studies and other research investigations accumulates over time. The discussion in this chapter of allocative, re-allocative, and innovative planning processes was designed to provide some conceptual structuring of these levels of planning.

To this point, this book has had relatively little to say about specific kinds of planning information or planning methodology. It is now time to turn to some of this material, which is the subject of Chapter 7.

7

Planning Resources
and Methodology

INTRODUCTION

This chapter reviews various kinds of resource materials and commentary that criminal justice planners can draw upon as they go about a specific planning task. We begin with some remarks about social process techniques that have been evolved for dealing with conflicts, disagreements, and points at issue among groups of persons who are embarked upon a deliberative planning process. These materials speak to the general question repeatedly asked by planners in the course of their work in carrying out some specific project: "How can I get all those people to agree on anything?" Some of these group process tactics can aid the planner in answering that question.

The second part of this chapter briefly examines a number

of quantitative tools that have been developed in recent years. In some of them, computer technology is put to work churning out information on the consequences that would ensue from one change or another introduced into some part of the justice system. We shall also look at some sources of baseline information in this section.

The third part of this chapter describes program evaluation methodology through which "feedback" on the effects (or lack of effects) of ongoing programs can be provided to planners and administrators.

As we have mentioned previously, this book is intended as a primer or sourcebook for planners rather than as a complex technical treatise. Accordingly, our observations in this chapter are designed to alert planners to the technical literature on planning methodology but do not constitute adequate substitutes for the materials in their original form. Stated differently, neophyte planners will learn enough about computer simulation, system-rates analysis, or the Delphi technique in this chapter to be able to gain some appreciation of the possible uses of these materials in their own work. This chapter, however, makes no attempt to provide a detailed description of the FORTRAN computer program that is involved in one simulation model, the details of social process techniques, or other methodological specifics. The reader will doubtless want to turn to the original sources for more information on many of these matters.

SOCIAL PROCESS SKILLS IN PLANNING

Social Process Analysis

Chapter 3 has already discussed value conflicts and ideological quarrels among different individuals and groups within the criminal justice system or within component parts of that machinery, and it specifically noted Walter Miller's observations on ideological perspectives, including some of his recommendations regarding techniques that could be used to reduce these value disagreements.[1] Miller advocates a search for and exposure of one's ideology, that is, one's gen-

---

[1] Walter B. Miller, "Ideology and Criminal Justice Policy: Some Current Issues," *Journal of Criminal Law and Criminology*, 64 (June 1973), 141–62.

eral and abstract beliefs or assumptions about the proper state of
things, which reflect, in turn, one's response to the moral order and
political arrangements that serve to shape one's position on specific
issues. In so doing, the planner may increase his or her capacity to
discriminate between those types of information that are more heavily
invested with ideological content and those that are less so. In other
words, this procedure may heighten the planner's ability to distinguish
between "fact" and "value" statements concerning the sources of
crime, the locus of responsibility, and also the modes of dealing with
crime in terms of policies with respect to offenders and criminal justice
agencies.

But even when the planner "gets his own head together" regarding an ideological posture, that person still must engage in interaction with individuals and groups and very often in situations where
conflict is close to or openly on the surface.

Unfortunately, social science research has not yet produced a
comprehensive, valid body of practice theory for planning, centering
on group process techniques. This gap in the knowledge base has been
noted by Callahan:

> At the present time, much of the knowledge base of social planning
> is a haphazard collection of practical principles and sundry truisms
> such as "Planning begins with dissatisfaction," "Participation of all
> important interests is necessary," "Involve the power structure," and
> "Obstacles to planning must be identified and overcome." Some
> attempts have been made to develop a theoretical base, and some
> principles are supported by empirical data gathered for the purpose,
> but in most cases this data is not substantial. Planners have hardly
> begun the long-term effort that will be required to identify the vari-
> ables that influence planning, to specify the types of relationships
> existing among the variables, and to create useful concepts that
> summarize and organize the variables and their relationships.[2]

Still, we are not entirely without useful knowledge regarding
social processes and social interaction that can be applied to conflict
resolution and other interactional issues that arise in planning.
Warren, for example, has provided an analysis of the "consensus dimension" in the community organization field, setting forth the

---

2 James J. Callahan, Jr., "Obstacles and Social Planning," *Social Work,*
18 (Winter 1973), 70–79.

hypothesis that the planner can make use of certain role techniques depending on the degree of consensus, differences, or outright disagreement existing in a particular situation.[3] In the first instance, where relative consensus exists, the planner will emphasize cooperation or collaboration. Where differences in opinion reign but potential for consensus is possible because polarization is not extreme, persuasion becomes a valid tactic. Finally, where issue dissensus is clear, the planner may have to develop alternate tactics and strategies from within or without his or her organization to obtain action.

These hypotheses are broad generalizations which are based largely on informal observation and limited research. For the most part, they parallel the empirical generalizations and action guidelines based upon them which Jack Rothman has assembled.[4] He is concerned primarily with providing a core of basic social science research knowledge to social planners and community workers in a variety of human services fields for use in guiding their strategies and action. The sense of Rothman's collation of research findings and action proposals can be gained from the following examples:

Generalization 4.10: The organization's dominant goals reflect the influence of the most powerful individuals or group in the organization and their vested interests.

Action guideline: Practitioners who wish to change organizational goals may approach this task by shifting the division of power in the organization, either by increasing the power of those groups which hold goals compatible with theirs, or introducing into the organization new groups, which have goals compatible with theirs.[5]

Generalization 6.24: Support by the chief executive is a critical factor in obtaining legislative approval of desired programs.

Action guideline: At the local level, as well as at the state level, for some types of issues (i.e., fluoridation) the most valuable support

---

[3] Roland L. Warren, "Types of Purposive Social Change at the Community Level," in Ralph M. Kramer and Harry Specht, eds., Readings in Community Organization Practice, 2nd ed. (Englewood Cliffs, N.J.: Prentice-Hall, 1975), pp. 134–49.

[4] Jack Rothman, Planning and Organization for Social Change (New York: Columbia University Press, 1974); also see Rothman, John L. Erlich, and Joseph G. Teresa, Promoting Innovation and Change in Organizations and Communities: A Planning Manual (New York: John Wiley, 1976).

[5] Rothman, Planning and Organization, pp. 135–37.

one can obtain is that of the chief executive. At the state level there is little question that the governor's support is a critical factor in respect to a range of issues. The practitioner should therefore be particularly alert for opportunities to obtain access to the chief executive. Particularly with regard to less popular issues (such as prison reform, welfare benefits, and abortion legislation) the support of the chief executive can spell the difference between success and failure.[6]

While the criminal justice planner will not find direct application for some of Rothman's volume, much of the material there is applicable to the criminal justice planning process.[7] At the same time, it is obvious enough that these propositions and guidelines are not as powerful as one might wish. It is not overly enlightening to be told that the governor may be a critical factor in obtaining legislative approval of controversial programs, but what is even more important, readers are likely to respond to some of these action guidelines by asking *how* they are to obtain the ear of the governor or *how* they might get more people into critical groups who share their goals and values. Stated another way, these action guidelines are relatively broad ones, rather than constituting specific recipes for problem solving. These are limitations of the social science fields from which Rothman has drawn, for which he cannot be held responsible.

Structured Process Techniques

Planning methods and techniques include what we term here *structured process techniques,* that is specific tactics or devices for obtaining information and data and for expediting the decision-making process. The more popular group facilitating processes include the *Delphi, Delbecq,* and *Mason* techniques. Simply stated, the Delphi

---

6 Ibid., pp. 245–46.

7 Also see Simon Slavin, "Concepts of Social Conflict: Use in Social Work Curricula," in Kramer and Specht, *Readings in Community Organization Practice,* pp. 364–78. Slavin treats social conflict from the perspective of the relevance of social work education. However, he stresses the positive and creative functions of conflict and suggests concepts for the analysis of conflict situations. While Slavin's presentation is focused on conflict emerging between individuals and groups on the community level, his hypothetical groupings of strategies have relevance for the criminal justice planner at the planning or operating agency level.

technique involves the presentation of additional input into the group decision-making process so that participants can reconsider and possibly revise their earlier estimates of a given problem, thus enabling the group to take into account considerations they might have neglected and to give due weight to factors they had previously dismissed as unimportant.[8] The Delbecq technique uses components of Delphi; however, it also stresses direct confrontation in that the experts are divided into small groups where they are pitted against one another in relation to the decisions they made involving crucial choice items.[9] Mason's dialectical approach addresses itself to the problem of selection among alternatives by the use of two different interpretations of the same planning data. Theoretically, in this approach, the proponents of each alternative are forced to look at the assumptions upon which their plan is based or expose those assumptions to verbal attack by their opponents. The expectation is that the result will be a new alternative, based upon assumptions from the previous two alternatives which are thought to be most valid.[10]

While techniques such as Delphi, Delbecq, and Mason might be useful to the planner who is both a novice in the field of criminal justice and inexperienced in group interactional processes, they have clear limitations when an "exercise" oportunity cannot be created or does not exist. The time and opportunity constraints faced by the planner frequently demand that he or she act alone and with whatever data can be assembled to deal with decision-making impasses or serious value conflicts.

Planning Roles

In addition to gaining as much understanding as possible regarding social interaction dynamics and processes, it is important that the criminal justice planner have a grasp of the various functional roles he or she can and does play in the planning process. For pur-

---

[8] Michael O'Neill, Ronald F. Bykowski, and Robert S. Blair, *Criminal Justice Planning: A Practical Approach* (San Jose, Calif.: Justice Systems Development, 1976), p. 89. Also see Andre L. Delbecq, Andrew H. Van de Ven, and David H. Gustafson, *Group Techniques for Program Planning: A Guide to Nominal Group and Delphi Processes* (Glenview, Ill.: Scott, Foresman, 1975).

[9] Ibid., p. 90.

[10] Richard O. Mason, "A Dialectical Approach to Strategic Planning," *Management Science*, 15 (April 1969), 403–14.

poses of this discussion, these are termed "interactional roles," since they identify the planner's multiple relationships with individuals in and out of the political system, with criminal justice agencies, and with policy, advisory, and community groups. In dealing with the wide range and degrees of dissensus (and consensus) among individuals, groups, and agencies, the planner will eventually identify a number of roles to play. These various roles and functions can be described as follows:

1. *Analyst-Synthesizer*
   The planner frequently analyzes nonquantified information inputs into the planning process, and when technical expertise is not available he or she is left with the task of analyzing data produced by the various justice agencies. Related to this task is often the important function of synthesizing the information and data inputs for presentation to advisory and policy groups, criminal justice agencies, community groups, and the public media.

2. *Communicator*
   The planner must be a communicator *par excellence,* developing formal and informal communication patterns with key actors among the political, community, advisory, and policy boards; with criminal justice agencies; and with community groups and the public media. Group and interpersonal communication skills are essential ingredients to the planner's ability to play the "linking" role in the complex planning process.

3. *Leader-Persuader-Motivator*
   Inevitably, at various points in the planning process, the planner must exercise a clear leadership role in his or her relationships with individuals and groups. In fact, the planner is often looked to by individuals and groups to provide direction and motivation. Not infrequently a planner's leadership will take the form of persuasion to move individuals and groups from noncommitment and "drift" to a specific focus and decision.

4. *Advocate*
   Planning by definition is a change process. The planner as advocate is a legitimate role when facts and circumstances warrant his or her expressions and when his or her knowledge

extends beyond that of individuals and groups. Stated another way, advocacy is compatible with the role of the professional planner defined as an individual who is not value-free and whose role is more than that of technical expert and executive secretary.

5. *Innovator-Strategist*

The planner frequently combines functions of innovator and strategist to deal with the multitude of substantive planning issues as well as the range of value conflicts inherent in the planning process. In his or her professional capacity, the planner is viewed as an "idea" person who also has an experientially based knowledge of how best to manage planning problems.

6. *Negotiator-Mediator*

At any point in the planning process, the planner may have to assume the role of negotiator or mediator. The fact that the planner is viewed by participating individuals and groups as having a certain "neutrality" in conflict situations makes one or another of these roles appropriate in given circumstances.

7. *Administrator-Implementer*

Depending on his or her position in an organizational arrangement, a planner may have to fulfill the role of agency, bureau, or unit administrator. Thus it is imperative that a planner have knowledge of administrative processes, since planning efforts reach into agency policymaking and operations. The implementing role may be less well defined but may well encompass involvement in details of plan implementation as well as implementation strategies.

This listing of role functions is by no means comprehensive, nor is it meant to imply that some roles are more important than others further down the list. The planner will wear a variety of hats, depending on the issues, circumstances, timing, and personalities involved in particular planning episodes, and all conditioned by his or her own estimation of how he or she can be most effective in the planning role. Interactional planning roles and functional strategies will be an ongoing subject of interest and concern to the planning theorist who sees the critical need to discover practice skills for their potential in making planning a more rational and effective process.

The criminal justice planner, whether in an operational or a planning agency position, can therefore identify with the urban planner's dilemma:

> With the multitude of roles and the complex array of skill dimensions, an urban planner is usually faced with an inability to assume all speaking parts in the play. Even assuming he had the skills, he would certainly find it impracticable to assemble the necessary resources. Thus, he is inevitably faced with the problem of coordinating and motivating others in their participation in the decision-making process.[11]

QUANTITATIVE TOOLS FOR JUSTICE PLANNING

Basic Resources

We have put considerable emphasis on the paucity of basic knowledge upon which criminal justice planning is based in the discussions to this point. That emphasis is reasonable enough, for justice planning is still in its infancy and in need of further nurturing. At the same time, it should be noted that there are more quantitative tools and resources now available, along with other helpful planning frameworks, than is sometimes acknowledged.

Leonard Oberlander has compiled a hefty volume published by LEAA of materials dealing with quantitative resources for planners.[12] That monograph contains essays by twenty-one different contributors. In one chapter of the volume, Oberlander and Blair Ewing

---

11 Richard S. Bolan, "Community Decision Behavior: The Culture of Planning," in Kramer and Specht, *Readings in Community Organization Practice*, pp. 150–74.

12 Leonard Oberlander, ed., *Quantitative Tools for Criminal Justice Planning* (Washington, D.C.: Law Enforcement Assistance Administration, 1975). For a compendium of criminal justice statistics of the kind described in the Oberlander volume, see Michael J. Hindelang, Christopher S. Dunn, Alison L. Aumick, and L. Paul Sutton, *Sourcebook of Criminal Justice Statistics, 1974* (Washington, D.C.: Law Enforcement Assistance Administration, 1975).

have provided a summary of the various kinds of data and methodological tools upon which planners might draw.[13]

One broad category of planning information noted by Oberlander and Ewing is data on crime, involving victimization surveys, *Uniform Crime Reports* statistics, "modus operandi" files, Offender-Based Transaction Statistics (OBTS), and other local crime data. A second general category of resource material deals with information on the criminal justice system and includes Offender-Based Transaction Statistics, as well as a variety of management and administrative data that can often be retrieved from the archives or files of specific agencies. (OBTS provides information both on crime and on the criminal justice machinery.)

The Offender-Based Transaction Statistics data system refers to longitudinal or tracking information compiled on individual offenders, in which the individual offender is the unit of count. He or she is followed through the justice system, and events occurring to him or her in component parts of the justice structure are systematically recorded.[14]

OBTS allows criminal activities to be analyzed with respect to individual offenders and with regard to offense. Data collected on a local level from the police, prosecutor's office, courts, and corrections are integrated for large areas in an attempt to produce a faster, more reliable and accurate picture of crime and its processing by the criminal justice system. Thus criminal activity can be described from the point of view of offenses. OBTS is designed to produce a demographic and criminal profile of offenders, a description of crime patterns, and identification of certain offender groups, and it is also a means of exploring the effects of various dispositions and correctional actions on rehabilitation and/or recidivism.

Data gathered through the OBTS method provide information on such questions as time variations in the processing of offenders, the extent of recirculation of offenders through the justice system, and the relationship between inputs at one stage and outputs at another. In short, the OBTS system produces information that is not

---

[13] Leonard Oberlander and Blair G. Ewing, "Quantitative Tools for Criminal Justice Planning," in Oberlander, *Quantitative Tools,* pp. 1–10.

[14] Susan Katzenelson, "Analysis of Crime with Offender Based Transaction Statistics (OBTS)," in Oberlander, *Quantitative Tools,* pp. 71–79. For a description of the OBTS system and an example of the actual use of it, see Carl E. Pope, *Offender-Based Transaction Statistics: New Directions in Data Collection and Reporting* (Washington, D.C.: Law Enforcement Assistance Administration, 1975).

available from more traditional recording systems that give us only summary descriptions of cohorts of offenders at specific points in the justice apparatus.

A third category of information consists of data on offender behavior, which involves such material as school truancy records and other school information on offenders, mental health reports, contact data from social services agencies, parallel reports from alcoholism and drug-abuse agencies in the community, and unemployment records on individuals available from employment offices. These authors also draw attention to a body of available information on the social environment, which includes population materials available from the U.S. Bureau of the Census and from such local agencies as the Center for Population and Research at Portland State University and the Center of Population Research at the University of Washington, as well as population figures gathered by the state agencies in California. Environmental information would also include various kinds of data on land use, land topography, land values, and so on, which are easily available in local communities. This kind of demographic and economic material is of inestimable value in preparing forecasts of criminal justice system work loads, analysis of crime patterns, and kindred planning assignments.[15]

Oberlander and Ewing identify a fourth category of quantitative resources in the form of methodological tools for processing and analyzing the kinds of data previously enumerated. They provide some brief commentary on various statistical techniques, along with a discussion of the JUSSIM model (Justice System Interactive Model), the PROMIS system (Prosecutor's Management Information System),

---

[15] We should also indicate that criminology textbooks represent a major resource for planners, as these works include relatively massive amounts of empirical evidence on crime patterns, offender behavior, and related matters. For example, see Don C. Gibbons, *Society, Crime, and Criminal Careers*, 3rd ed. (Englewood Cliffs, N.J.: Prentice-Hall, 1977); and Gibbons, *Delinquent Behavior*, 2nd ed. (Englewood Cliffs, N.J.: Prentice-Hall, 1976).

In addition, the resourceful planner can find a large variety of other material of considerable value in planning. See Calvin F. Schmid and Stanton E. Schmid, *Crime in the State of Washington* (Olympia: Law and Justice Planning Office, Washington State Planning and Community Affairs Agency, 1972) for an example of a university-produced compilation of useful crime data. Also see Thomas A. Reppetto, *Residential Crime* (Cambridge, Mass.: Ballinger, 1974) for an example of a basic research study on patterns of burglary that would be of great utility in efforts at crime-based planning; and Harry A. Scarr, Joan L. Pinsky, and Deborah S. Wyatt, *Patterns of Burglary* (Washington, D.C.: Law Enforcement Assistance Administration, 1973).

and geocoding of crime information. We will return to a discussion of the JUSSIM model later in this chapter.

The Oberlander volume contains much information of value to the justice planner who is casting about for a data base and methodological techniques to employ in planning. At the same time, this monograph says something about the present underdeveloped state of the art in planning. For example, one chapter deals with Uniform Crime Reports information compiled by the Federal Bureau of Investigation, pointing out the ways in which these data can be used in planning. But it does not mention the many problems that continue to plague these statistics, including those revolving around police department manipulation of crime statistics.[16] Along the same line, another chapter presents a discussion of prediction of crime incidence and estimation of changes in crime rates that is based on relatively complex statistical procedures. Although the statistical techniques are quite detailed and technical, the underlying argument is quite crude and simple, namely, that current trends will continue into the future. Little or no attention is given in these efforts to identifying the underlying reasons for current patterns of crime or to assessing the likelihood that crime-producing conditions will remain constant, so that it is difficult to know whether any confidence can be placed in these statistical extrapolations.

System Rates

The work of Malcolm Klein, Solomon Kobrin, A. W. McEachern, Herbert Sigurdson, Robert Carter, and Cameron Dightman regarding system rates represents a body of analysis that is of considerable utility in justice planning.[17] In the main essay in which

---

[16] See Gibbons, *Society, Crime, and Criminal Careers;* Marvin E. Wolfgang, "Uniform Crime Reports: A Critical Appraisal," *University of Pennsylvania Law Review,* April 1963, pp. 708–38; David Seidman and Michael Couzens, "Getting the Crime Rate Down: Political Pressure and Crime Reporting," *Law and Society Review,* 8 (Spring 1974), 457–93; and Michael Hindelang, "The Uniform Crime Report Revisited," *Journal of Criminal Justice,* 1 (Spring 1974), 1–18.

[17] Malcolm W. Klein, Solomon Kobrin, A. W. McEachern, and Herbert Sigurdson, "System Rates: An Approach to Comprehensive Criminal Justice Planning," *Crime and Delinquency,* 17 (October 1971), 365–72; Herbert Sigurdson, Robert Carter, and A. W. McEachern, "Methodological Impediments to Comprehen-

system rates analysis is described, Klein, Kobrin, McEachern, and Sigurdson point out that the current criminal justice machinery is in actuality a nonsystem that cries out for comprehensive planning around some form of system analysis. They also note that comprehensive planning is often made difficult or impossible by the lack of adequate longitudinal data tracing the flow of offenders through the parts of the system.[18] It is that deficiency that system rates analysis is designed to remedy.

System rates are specific numerical indicators of the proportion of individuals who receive a particular service or who are the targets of some identifiable justice system decision, contrasted to the total number of persons eligible for that service or decision. For example, a community absorption rate would be one showing the number of juveniles who are turned back into the community without official police action, divided by the total number of youths falling into the hands of the police. Similarly, a probation processing rate would be one showing the proportion of probationers among convicted persons. Klein and his coauthors note six types of system rates: community absorption rates, apprehension rates, processing rates, release rates, reabsorption rates, and recidivism rates. The underlying logic of system rates and that of the OBTS scheme is essentially the same.

Klein and his associates argue that identification of system rates for the various decision points within the criminal and juvenile justice system has major implications for planning:

> The criminal justice system, to the detriment of both society and the offender population, does not currently operate as a truly functional independent system. It is not sufficiently integrated with respect to public agencies and community resources. It does not yet have an effective means for assessing its own status or its impact on crime and delinquency. It requires a systematic procedure for comprehensive planning as a forerunner to comprehensive modification (emphasis added).[19]

---

sive Criminal Justice Planning," *Criminology,* 9 (August–November 1971), 248–67; Robert Carter, Cameron R. Dightman, and Malcolm W. Klein, "The System Rate Approach to Description and Evaluation of Criminal Justice Systems: An Illustration," *Criminology,* 11 (February 1974), 462–83.

[18] Klein, Kobrin, McEachern, and Sigurdson, "System Rates," pp. 357–58.

[19] Ibid., p. 361.

Broadly stated, identification of system rates constitutes the basic operation of "getting the facts" regarding the workings of the justice machinery upon which comprehensive planning can then proceed. The next step revolves around identification of the determinants responsible for the rates of police diversion of juveniles, prosecutorial decisions to dismiss certain cases, judicial decisions to sentence to probation, and other system activities expressed collectively as rates. These authors also indicate that rate determinants are quite varied, so that some center on statutory and community definitions of deviant behavior, while others involve the levels of lawbreaking behavior in the community. Other rate determinants are linked to variations in community resources, community attitudes, system philosophies, system effectiveness, and community-system coordination. Stated another way, few offenders may be placed on probation in a specific community, for example, because that community is lacking in community agency resources, because of negative judicial attitudes toward probation, or because most offenders who are convicted in court are recidivists and inappropriate candidates for release into the community. Other examples come readily to mind.

Klein and his associates are quite persuasive in enumerating a series of positive functions of system rates analysis. These rates allow us to assess the current efficiency of component parts of the justice apparatus, as well as to identify changes that have occurred over time. These rates also focus attention on parts of the overall system that may be amenable to positive change, and they also provide us with a device for gauging the extent to which planned changes have produced the anticipated effects.

Several comments are in order regarding the system rates (and OBTS) approach to justice planning. First, there is little question that a detailed system rates description of the workings of a particular justice system in a specific jurisdiction would provide a valuable body of *baseline data* on which the planning process might proceed. Surely no one would argue that planning can operate effectively out of ignorance regarding the current workings of the system that is to be the target for planned change. Second, the basic idea of system rates is a straightforward one, although the development of a full statement of system rates in a specific community or jurisdiction would often be a relatively difficult task. Reduced to essentials, system rates analysis is a more detailed version of the descriptions of the flow of offenders through the justice system found in criminology textbooks.[20] Third, system rates analysis has been utilized, at least in rudimentary form, both in an illustrative examination of the work-release program in Washington State[21] and in a jail planning study in the state of Oregon.[22] In the latter case, a compilation of data dealing with misdemeanant and felony offenders and decision points in the processing of these persons was assembled so that informed planning could be undertaken in the direction of jail reforms and the development of alternatives to jailing in that state.

The major point to be made about system rates analysis is that while this technique is valuable for producing baseline data for planning purposes, it is not necessarily true, contrary to the authors' opinion, that "new action programs, changes in administrative procedures, and new legislative needs would emerge almost automatically from this process."[23] The identification of system rates and rate determinants would suggest some of these planning directions, but *the basic planning task has only been started at that point.* Even beyond the tremendously complex problem of developing and keeping updated a system rates data bank, crucial and equally or more difficult planning issues will arise within the boundaries of the pluralistic decision-making process that involves legislators, local politicians, members of the public, and other influence groups. Planning experience clearly indicates that actions to implement policy decisions do not inevitably occur once those logical recommendations based on relatively sound data have been produced. Thus, while Klein and his coauthors have made an excellent case for a system rates data base for planning purposes, any optimism about the ultimate payoff of such a system should be seen in the context of the much more complex planning arena.

---

[20] For a presentation of system processing of juvenile offenders, see Gibbons, *Delinquent Behavior*, pp. 16–34; for a discussion of system processing of adult offenders, see Gibbons, *Society, Crime, and Criminal Careers*, pp. 81–84, 105–24, 479–83.

[21] Carter, Dightman, and Klein, "System Rate Approach."

[22] Don C. Gibbons, *District 9 Correctional Feasibility Study, Summary and Recommendations* (Salem: State of Oregon, Corrections Division, 1971).

[23] Klein, Kobrin, McEachern, and Sigurdson, "System Rates," p. 372.

System Analysis and the JUSSIM Model

Another analytic scheme which is quite similar to the system rates approach can be found in the work of Alfred Blumstein and others. In one essay, Blumstein and Richard Larson presented a complex mathematical model of the justice system operation in California which identifies agency costs, work loads, and the flow of offenders through the system.[24] One problem with Blumstein and Larson's scheme is that utilization of it requires an understanding of fairly complex mathematical skills. More importantly, the Blumstein-Larson model is derived from *internal* measures of system performance and does not take into account such external factors as legislative decisions, community demands, and interagency competition, which must be dealt with in comprehensive justice planning.

The system modeling of Blumstein led to the development of the JUSSIM model (Justice System Interactive Model).[25] The JUSSIM model is a FORTRAN computer program into which information on offender flows through the parts of the correctional machinery is pumped, along with data on agency work loads, agency resources, and unit costs for processing offenders. The computer program provides answers to such questions as "What if we were to release 10 percent more of all convicted offenders into probation programs?" or "What will the consequences be of a 20 per cent reduction in jail populations in this jurisdiction?" The computer is able to provide detailed answers based upon the system-processing information that was previously put into it.

The JUSSIM model is a planning tool for the analysis of the impact of alternative choices in that when a proposed system change is to be considered, estimates of parameter effects of that change are derived from the computer. The JUSSIM model provides the basis for translating a programmatic change in the criminal justice system

---

[24] Alfred Blumstein and Richard Larson, "Models of a Total Criminal Justice System," *Operations Research*, 17 (March–April 1969), 199–232.

[25] The JUSSIM model is presented in detail in Alfred Blumstein, "A Model to Aid in Planning for the Total Criminal Justice System," in Oberlander, *Quantitative Tools*, pp. 129–61; and Jacqueline Cohen, Kenneth Fields, Michele Lettre, Richard Stafford, and Claire Walker, "Implementation of the JUSSIM Model in a Criminal Justice Planning Agency," *Journal of Research in Crime and Delinquency*, 25 (July 1973), 117–31.

to an estimate of the impact of that change on performance measures of the system. The computer is used in an "interactive" mode, with the user calling a stored data base characterizing his or her criminal justice system and interacting in a conversational way with the computer program.

In large part, the JUSSIM model differs from system rates analysis only in the use of computer technology. Both of these techniques provide relatively elaborate indications of the likely consequences that will ensue from some change in one part or another of the justice system. In the case of the JUSSIM computer program, we are able to employ the marvels of the computer age to obtain detailed and precise answers to system-impact questions. At the same time, we would reiterate that the basic idea that changes in one part of the machinery ramify to other parts is not a novel one. Further, we need to repeat that computers can only offer responses in terms of information that is put into the computer. What the JUSSIM model cannot do is to provide us with guidance on how to deal with legislatures and quarrelsome legislators, community pressures and demands, and some of the other field forces that play upon the criminal justice machinery. These comments are not intended to denigrate the importance of system rates analysis or the JUSSIM model, but only to caution against undue optimism regarding the planning miracles that might be wrought by computers!

Other Approaches

The Prosecutors Management Information System (PROMIS) is another crime-oriented tool that can be utilized by planners. PROMIS, which contains many of the data concerned for inclusion in the OBTS, specifically permits a prosecutor's office to accumulate information on each case and to receive reports and analyses based on these data so that prosecutors can identify and concentrate on priority areas. It contains relevant information on the workings and decisions of the court process from arrest through final dispositions.[26]

Another discussion of planning involves the work of John Tropman and and Karl Gohlke and centers on cost-benefit analysis of

---

[26] Sidney Brounstein and William Hamilton, "Analysis of the Criminal Justice System with the Prosecutors Management Information System," in Oberlander, *Quantitative Tools*, pp. 91–111.

justice system operations.[27] Their commentary is quite general, and more sophisticated discussions of cost-benefit techniques in measurement of correctional endeavors are available.[28] However, the central point to be made about cost-benefit analysis is that it is a useful means of obtaining *baseline data for planning*, even though it does not deal with the system change problems which represent the core task of planning. In other words, cost-benefit analysis, while often critical to the decision-making process, is essentially some further informational input that allows for important comparisons of programs and various alternatives. Like the system rates approach of Klein noted above, cost-benefit analysis has merit in terms of contributing a further informational dimension to the planning process, even though it may not necessarily lead to the positive correlation that one would expect to see between reasonably valid data and rational decision making. The more complicated planning function remains that of utilizing quantifiable data in the planning marketplace where the participants very often behave on the basis of unquantifiable considerations springing from values, preferences, ideologies, and politics.

The conclusion that can be drawn from the discussion of quantitative tools to this point, and particularly those advocated by LEAA, is that they are designed to produce information such as impact of proposed changes within the current system, along with identification of high-incidence crime areas and the characteristics of a particular offense, the offender, and also his victim. This crime-oriented approach views crime as the problem, not those factors that cause crime. It centers on more efficient control of crime based upon a more efficient response of the criminal justice system to specific crimes. This approach does not emphasize the study of crime as a dependent variable strongly influenced by the social environment. From a planning perspective, these quantitative approaches can be considered as focused on improvement of the present system. They are probably most useful in incremental criminal justice system planning rather than comprehensive planning that views crime as a product of many social, economic, and institutional variables.

Berkowitz presents an alternative model, the community assessment approach to criminal justice planning. From the results of in-

---

[27] John E. Tropman and Karl H. Gohlke, "Cost/Benefit Analysis—Comprehensive Planning in the Criminal Justice System," *Crime and Delinquency*, 18 (July 1973), 315–22.

[28] Daniel Glaser, *Routinizing Evaluation* (Rockville, Md.: National Institute of Mental Health, 1975).

vestigations suggesting that basic socioeconomic factors promote the incidence of crime, she goes on to call for a data base for planning that integrates crime data with census data.[29] This would allow the criminal justice planner to explore the relationship between the incidence of crime and socioeconomic variables as well as other factors concerning the nature and quality of life in the community. She holds that this approach is most promising in that many variables that prior research has found to be highly associated with crime rates have also been shown to be highly associated with each other. Furthermore, the community assessment model permits testing of hypotheses about the causation of crime through use of a methodology (multiple factor approach) that tackles portions of the universe of crime-related and demographic variables and reduces them to groups of variables of manageable size for factor analysis. The combined use of factor analysis and cluster analysis (from social area analysis) is designed to identify and study in greater detail the specific social processes that produce variations in crime rates. In turn, this information would provide the planner with clues regarding effective programs for crime prevention and reduction. Berkowitz also believes that ecological studies of crime can be instructive in efforts to demonstrate the limitations of existing theories concerning individual attributes and crime, particularly if extensive data from victimization surveys are incorporated so as to avoid the fallacy of developing hypotheses about the causes of crime that are based on only official offenses and offenders.[30]

FORECASTING THE FUTURE: POPULATION, SOCIAL AND ECONOMIC TRENDS, AND CRIMINALITY

We have alluded earlier to the matter of population, economic, and crime forecasting, and to some of the difficulties involved in that enterprise. Let us offer a few more observations on that topic.

---

[29] Francine Berkowitz, "The Community Assessment Approach to Criminal Justice Planning: An Alternative Model," California Council on Criminal Justice (7171 Bowling Drive, Sacramento, n.d.), pp. 13–23.

[30] Ecological studies of crime and delinquency, along with various statistical techniques such as correlational analysis and social area analysis used in ecological studies, are reviewed in Gibbons, *Delinquent Behavior*, pp. 105–14.

The criminal justice planner must grapple with the future by endeavoring to divine some of the major social, demographic, economic, and political events that are likely to affect criminal justice practice in five years, a decade, or a longer period into the future. However, the observation has been made that planners for the most part have only attempted to extend plans a few years into the future and have sloughed off the task of forecasting coming developments, assuming, implicitly or explicitly, that current conditions will continue unchanged. However, a moment's reflection should indicate that this is an unlikely assumption. This is a time when rapid changes are occurring in nearly every dimension of modern life. Alvin Toffler, in *Future Shock,* has popularized the thesis that we are in danger of being engulfed by social changes taking place at ever-increasing rates.[31]

Now, it is easy enough to argue that criminal justice planning is a form of futurology, in which comprehensive plans must be created on the basis of prognostications of coming developments, but it is quite another thing to identify these trends with any degree of certainty. In the following paragraphs some of the major dimensions of the predictive problem in criminal planning are considered.

The easiest forecasting task centers on demographic trends. Straightforward techniques exist for estimating the size and composition of the national or state populations for a number of decades into the future. Demographic prediction proceeds in this manner: current data on birth and death rate levels are assembled, along with quantified conjectures about expected migration into and out of the area in question. These population measures are then coupled with assumptions about birth rates, death rates, and migration levels in the future and are applied to current population figures, with the end product being specific estimates of future population levels. Although population processes have sometimes undergone sharp and rapid changes, invalidating the assumptions on which forecasts have been based and thus resulting in unpredicted population changes, such occurrences have been more the exception than the rule.[32] As a result, population forecasts often have the appearance of hard facts.

Turning to population projections for coming decades, while 20- to 29-year-old males made up 6.9 percent of the total population

---

[31] Alvin Toffler, *Future Shock* (New York: Random House, 1970).

[32] The most well known case in point involves the national population forecasts prepared by demographers in the period before World War II, predicting negligible population growth in the 1950s. These forecasts were based on the assumption that prewar birth rates would continue unchanged and did not anticipate the "baby boom" of the 1950s.

of 2,091,385 persons in Oregon in 1970, it is estimated that this group will comprise 9.2 percent of the state population of over 2,800,000 individuals in 1985. Males in this age group will increase from 144,300 in 1970 to over 260,000 in 1985.[33]

It seems a safe prediction that property crime rates will remain reasonably high in Oregon through at least 1985, given these population trends. That is, "garden-variety" property offenses are predominantly the work of young males in their twenties, and it can be seen from these population forecasts that such individuals will constitute an increased portion of the total population in 1985.

But planning requires more than crude predictions that crime levels will remain "reasonably high." How high is reasonably high? It is at this point in the practice of futurology that a good deal of difficulty and uncertainty in prognostications is experienced.

It is possible to generate more precise estimates of the levels of crime to be expected in the future. For example, Kelly Hancock and Don Gibbons have applied age-specific national arrest rates for 1974 reported in FBI statistics to population forecasts for the year 2050.[34] Their calculations indicate that while there were 2,164,100 arrests in 1974 for Index crimes, there will be 2,344,789 arrests for those offenses in 2050. Larceny arrests will increase from 1,056,300 in 1974 to 1,125,353 in 2050, while robbery arrests will grow from 148,720 to 159,714. Similar increases are projected for the other index offenses.

Should these projections be taken seriously? These predictions are precise, but are they *accurate?* Are crime levels in 2050 likely to be lower than predicted or will they be markedly higher? Obviously, a heavy measure of guesswork would go into any answer that is provided to questions such as these. However, the more reasonable guess is that these forecasts *underestimate* the amount of crime likely to be observed in 2050.

The reasoning, sketched out here in only its barest outlines, proceeds along the following lines.[35] First, it is well established that property crimes among young adult males occur most frequently in

---

[33] These population estimates were produced by the Center for Population Research and Census, Portland State University.

[34] R. Kelly Hancock and Don C. Gibbons, "The Future of Crime in American Society" (unpublished).

[35] One assumption implicit in these figures is that the ratio of police arrests to the volume of crime will remain virtually unchanged in the future. If this assumption is in error, it is most likely to be faulty in the direction of underestimating the increase that may take place in police efficiency. If so, the crime estimates here would be underinflated rather than overinflated.

periods of high unemployment.[36] James Levine has reported that the correlation between robbery rates and the number of out-of-school and unemployed males in the 16- to 21-year-old category in the twenty-six largest cities in the country in 1970 was $r = .76$,[37] while Llad Phillips, Harold Votey, and Harold Maxwell have indicated that property crime rates are strongly correlated in inverse fashion with labor force participation on the part of 18- to 19-year-old males.[38] In short, these studies report consistent findings regarding the impact of unemployment on crime rates.

Also to be considered are official arrest statistics, which indicate that crime rates are much higher for blacks than for whites for a variety of offenses, particularly for garden-variety crimes included as Index crimes. The usual assumption is that the major explanation for these higher rates centers on the particularly disadvantaged position of blacks reflected in their employment and economic status.

A major premise in the argument holding that crime levels will continue to increase to 2050 is that unemployment among black and white males will persist at levels at least as high as currently observed. A whole set of additional assumptions about the economic well-being of the nation in the decades ahead is bound up with this premise about economic precariousness among American youth.

Space again limits the ability to spell out the details of the relatively gloomy conjectures about the deteriorated state of the American economy which is foreseen in the years ahead.[39] Also, space limitations preclude examination of the available evidence that can be brought to bear upon such questions as whether economic inequality between blacks and whites is being reduced or is remaining stable [40] or upon other questions regarding economic changes that are occurring or are in prospect for the United States. Moreover, this book is not

---

[36] Daniel Glaser and Kent Rice, "Crime, Age and Employment," *American Sociological Review,* 24 (October 1959), 679–86.

[37] James P. Levine, "The Ineffectiveness of Adding Police to Prevent Crime," *Public Policy,* 23 (Fall 1975), 136.

[38] Llad Phillips, Harold L. Votey, Jr., and Harold Maxwell, "Crime, Youth, and the Labor Market," *Journal of Political Economy,* 80 (May–June 1972), 491–503.

[39] This argument is presented in Hancock and Gibbons, "Future of Crime."

[40] Much of that evidence is reviewed in William J. Chambliss and Thomas E. Ryther, *Sociology* (New York: McGraw-Hill, 1975); Charles H. Anderson, *The Political Economy of Social Class* (Englewood Cliffs, N.J.: Prentice-Hall, 1974); Wayne J. Villemez and Alan R. Row, "Black Economic Gains in the Sixties: A Methodological Critique and Reassessment," *Social Forces,* 54 (September 1975), 181–93; and Sidney Willhelm, *Who Needs the Negro?* (Cambridge: Schenkman, 1970).

concerned with making a case for any particular vision of the future. Rather, the central conclusion to be drawn from the sketchy discussion here on forecasting social trends and criminality is that such a venture is fraught with uncertainty. As one moves from predictions about population levels to be anticipated in future years to conjectures about levels of crime to be experienced, crime estimates must be produced despite the uncertainty regarding the factors that lie behind currently observed levels of lawbreaking. Moreover, even if it were possible to be more certain of our understanding of present-day crime, the same could not be said about estimates of impending changes in social and economic relationships.[41] A final, related point has to do with the need for theoreticians within justice planning. A constant theme running through this book is that the single most important ingredient of criminal justice planning knowledge is theoretical wisdom. We do not regard *theoretical* as a pejorative term; instead, we hold that one cannot deal adequately with questions of causation, viable responses to lawbreaking, or the future of crime in modern society unless that person is grounded in the theoretical perspectives and research evidence of the basic disciplines. The planner will never become an omniscient seer, but his or her predictions about the future are likely to be most accurate insofar as they are *informed* ones, derived from current social science findings.

EVALUATION AND THE PLANNING PROCESS

The Need for Evaluation Research

We argued in Chapter 6 that long-range and comprehensive criminal justice planning must out of necessity involve ongoing evaluation of programs. Researchers and practitioners alike in recent years have stressed the importance both of the evaluation of ongoing pro-

---

[41] One other question about the future has not been examined in this book but would be of concern to a criminal justice planner: What role is the federal government going to play in crime fighting in the next several years, the next decade, or beyond? Federal funding of criminal justice activities, through the Omnibus Crime Control and Safe Streets Act of 1968 and LEAA, increased from $63 million in 1969 to over $800 million in 1975. LEAA spending was at a somewhat reduced level in 1976, with proposed budgets for 1977 and later years showing further cutbacks of federal spending in this area. The crime-fighting industry grew correlatively with the

grams and of the use of evaluation results in order to help frame the direction of future programming.

The reasons for this emphasis on research evaluation of programs are not hard to find. For the most part, they center on the growing financial strains experienced by local and state governments and by the federal government as well. Governmental officials and legislators at all levels are beginning to demand hard evidence of the effectiveness of programs and are becoming increasingly restive about pouring funds into programs of indeterminate impact. In short, human services administrators and criminal justice agency heads have become attuned to a search for evidence of program impact in considerable part because they are being barraged by insistent demands to do so by taxpayers and legislators.

Those more concerned with a visionary planning process address themselves to structural changes in society so that we can become an experimenting society—one that makes decisions related to the most accurate data available. Planners and researchers such as Friedmann, Michael, and Campbell have addressed themselves to this phase of the evaluation process. For example, Friedmann writes that "evaluation must be expanded to mean a journey of exploration into the potential value field of a society." [42] He argues that because we know relatively little about the probable consequences of actions, except in certain restricted areas of behavior, we must identify entire value regions and use them in judging the significance of the data collected. In this way, exploratory evaluations point to value issues that must be confronted, which may in turn lead to redirection of social patterns and processes.

In his volume on long-range social planning, Michael states that evaluation—that is, the continuous assessment of the relevance of chosen goals and the effectiveness of programs underway in the pursuit of them—must be a central and continuing part of the planning process.[43] He considers it necessary to evaluate evaluation methods and

---

growth of federal spending. It seems obvious enough that if the federal government retreats markedly from crime control activities, criminal justice programs will be significantly reduced at the state and local levels, quite apart from any reductions or increases in levels of crime that are observed in states or local jurisdictions. At this writing in late 1976, with an impending presidential election, the issue of future federal spending is surely one for which no clear answers are available.

[42] John Friedmann, *Retracking America* (Garden City, N.Y.: Anchor Books/Doubleday, 1973), p. 214.

[43] Donald N. Michael, *On Learning to Plan—And Planning to Learn* (San Francisco: Jossey-Bass, 1973), pp. 64–67.

the purposes of evaluation themselves in order to learn how, when, and what to evaluate. He also stresses that the purpose of evaluation is not only to gather data and test hypotheses but should include a means by which "experimenters" and "subjects" alike learn new norms and behavior. In this view, evaluation is one part of long-range social planning, or what he terms "future-responsive social learning." Michael argues that we are going to have to learn to live with high levels of uncertainty, share information, and embrace errors as a learning experience. Evaluation research represents one tool among many to be employed in the planning-learning process.

Campbell views evaluation research as a means by which we can vigorously try out solutions to recurrent problems so that outcomes will lead to continued support of good programs or the movement toward viable alternatives.[44] He envisions a change in the thinking of the entire society whereby government planners will be able to accept critical comments and negative findings and be willing to change in the face of new evidence. Like Friedmann and Michael, Campbell sees the expanded use of evaluation as linked to reeducation and relearning on the part of the citizenry so that they will be able to pressure or support elected officials who move toward a questioning attitude rather than the usual simplistic attempts at resolution of social problems.

While not specifically concerned with the uses of program evaluation in planning, Lerman's *Community Treatment and Social Control* clearly demonstrates the necessity for a systems approach to the evaluation of results of new policies or programs. In his reevaluation of the results of the California Treatment Project and the Probation Subsidy Program, he found that these highly regarded programs turned out to be more costly and no more effective than traditional programs.[45] The wards in the experimental community caseloads in the California Treatment Project experienced more "social control" (detention) than "treatment" from their parole agents, despite the opposite intentions of the program's designers. Additional evidence indicates that the probation subsidy was associated with longer institutional stays at a state level and more frequent use of detention at a local level. Lerman therefore concludes that a narrow preoccupation

---

[44] Donald T. Campbell, in a conversation with Carol Travis, "The Experimenting Society: To Find Programs That Work, Government Must Measure Its Failures," *Psychology Today*, 9 (September 1975), 47–56.

[45] Paul Lerman, *Community Treatment and Social Control* (Chicago: University of Chicago Press, 1975).

with data relevant only for assessing achievement of the manifest goals of a project may lead to erroneous policy judgments. In essence, he urges a deliberate search for evidence of unintended consequences and accommodations within the project and in other parts of the system that may serve to enhance or subvert project objectives.

Evaluation Research Methodology

One relatively comprehensive statement on program evaluation in criminal justice has been offered by Don Gibbons, Barry Lebowitz, and Gerald Blake.[46] They note that much of the available literature on program evaluation is overly technical and argue that the basic problems and principles of program evaluation can be discussed in plain language.

In many real-life instances of evaluation research, the researcher is faced with assessment of an ill-defined program about which there is scanty information. The initial tasks thus is one of determining whether an evaluation is both feasible and warranted. This assessment involves at least the following determinations: (1) that procedures and objectives of the program can be defined and measured, (2) that linkages between program expenditures and activities can be identified, and (3) that the sponsors are willing and able to discuss their needs and expectations from the evaluation. If evaluative studies are not able to address these matters, most of them will probably result in information of dubious validity and of little or no utility to anyone.

The goals of ongoing correctional programs are often inchoate. Therefore, the first task often is one of clarifying the nature of the program to be evaluated, with measurement activities coming later. The simple fact is that many correctional endeavors have emerged haphazardly, without any clear theoretical rationale. Programs have sprung up in response to the latest fad, such as "community treatment," "group counseling," or "behavior modification." Those who started such programs lacked a clear sense of what they were trying to

---

[46] Don C. Gibbons, Barry D. Lebowitz, and Gerald F. Blake, "Program Evaluation in Correction," *Crime and Delinquency*, 22 (July 1976), 309–21. Some of the same points, as well as observations on the staffing and funding of program evaluation activities, appear in Gibbons, "The Administrator's Role in Research, Staffing, and Funding: Choosing an Evaluation Team and Anticipating Cost and Time Frame" (Paper presented at the First Annual Conference on Assessment and Evaluation, University of North Dakota, June 21, 1976).

do, and succeeding groups of employees have failed to articulate an explicit sense of program mission. Or, in other instances, those who began or implemented a particular type of organization may have had some implicit theoretical notions on which they based the program, but that structure has remained implicit. Accordingly, it becomes the task of the researcher to identify the nature of the activity to be evaluated.

Three interrelated aspects of the problem-defining task can be identified. First, the *image of the offender* upon which the program operates must be clarified. What kind of characterization of lawbreakers and lawbreaking is involved in it? Second, the *intervention tactic(s)* must be specified. All kinds of activities are centered on offenders in agencies, but the question is, Which of these agency operations are directly intended to have some effect upon lawbreakers? Stated another way, What endeavors is the program engaged in that are designed to modify or alter some of the "problems" identified in the image of the offender upon which the agency operates? Third, the *expected outcome* of intervention must be determined. The most obvious intended outcome is some degree of reduced recidivism. How much recidivism reduction is expected? Then, too, there are problems involved in defining recidivism and how it is to be measured. Finally, there is the question of whether recidivism rates ought to be used as the only measure of program success.

Once the problem-defining task has been accomplished, the general outlines of the research task become fairly obvious. Program evaluation endeavors become focused on three basic questions directed at the agency:

1. Do the agency "clients" really look like you thought they would?

2. Did you do what you said you were going to do, in the way of program efforts?

3. Did what you did with the offenders have any effect upon them?

Evaluation of ongoing correctional programs comes down to three interrelated assessments. The first has to do with determining whether the offenders being dealt with by the organization actually do fit the image of them that is implicit in the program. In the research literature, this stage is often called *effectiveness evaluation*. This work centers on collection and analysis of data on such variables as the target population, ease of access of the program to the target group, amount of information about the program in the community-at-large, and the proficiency of outreach or case finding and tracking.

The second evaluative assessment has to do with measuring the extent to which the correctional program actually did involve the intervention efforts that were intended to be applied to the offenders. Here the research job is one of data retrieval regarding such things as the number of times particular offenders received job counseling, emergency financial aid, group therapy, or some other form of assistance. Evaluation efforts of this form center on analysis of service delivery itself. Questions are raised concerning the capacity of the program to meet its goals, the degree to which staff members possess the necessary intervention skills, the training of the personnel, the attitudes and prejudices of the treatment agents concerning the recipients of the service, and the costs of the components of the program. All these questions are usually involved in an assessment of the *effiency* of a particular intervention operation.

Finally, what of the third form of assessment—measurement of program outcome? One piece of advice to program evaluators is that they should strive assiduously to avoid playing tricks on themselves, by glossing over or ignoring information that points to program failure. Paul Lerman has had much to say about the research pitfalls that some program evaluators have fallen into, as they have neglected to count persons who "fail to complete treatment"—i.e., dropouts—as failures, or in other ways have been less than scrupulously objective in marshaling all the evidence on a particular program.[47]

Gibbons, Lebowitz, and Blake have described three types or levels of evaluation: *effectiveness* (Who is being reached by the program?), *efficiency* (How is the program actually operating?), and *impact* (What are the social and economic benefits of the program?). It is important to recognize that attention must be paid to all three in a true evaluation study, for there is no necessary relationship among them. For example, a program might be beneficial to the people receiving the service, but these may not be the persons for whom the program was developed. Or, a highly efficient program, and especially one with low costs, may have low impact. It is common to equate efficiency, effectiveness, and impact, but the results of a one-dimen-

---

[47] Paul Lerman, "Evaluative Studies of Institutions for Delinquents: Implications for Research and Social Policy," *Social Work*, 13 (July 1968), 55–64.

sional evaluation can be highly misleading, with unwarranted conclusions being drawn from it.[48]

We have discussed the interrelatedness of evaluation and the
planning process in this section. Various authors have addressed this
issue in relation to both the primary planning process and the more
pragmatic aspects involved in program evaluation and comprehensive
planning. There is little question that research and evaluation have
been understressed in the LEAA planning process. This is extremely
unfortunate in view of the millions of dollars that have been spent
on criminal justice programs since 1968. However, the need for and
importance of research and evaluation even at this late date is essential if the comprehensive planning and goal-setting strategy now being
emphasized by LEAA is to be a consistent one. Selectivity as to what
is to be evaluated and the evaluation methodologies applied will continue because of the thousands of projects funded annually by LEAA,
but research and evaluation can no longer be passed off with lip service if LEAA's renewed stress on accountability is to be heeded by
state and local planning groups.

SUMMARY

It should be obvious from this chapter that criminal justice planning theorists are just beginning to accumulate the knowledge resources required for comprehensive planning. A knowledge base of
planning does exist, both in terms of the interactional roles implicit
in the planning process and in terms of the more structured measurement techniques available from other fields and under development
in one or another part of the criminal justice system. The immediate
task for criminal justice planners, therefore, would appear to be an
effort to absorb what can be learned from other planning areas and
apply that material when and where appropriate to the criminal

---

[48] We have avoided discussion of technical details of evaluation methodol-
ogy in this book. For a detailed, comprehensive bibliography on program evaluation
in corrections, see Florence Yospe, ed., *Program Evaluation in Corrections: An An-
notated Bibliography*, National Criminal Justice Educational Development Project,
Urban Studies Graduate Program, Portland State University, 1975. Also see Donald
R. Weidman, John D. Waller, Dona MacNeil, Francine L. Tolson and Joseph S. Wholey,
Intensive Evaluation for Criminal Justice Planning Agencies (Washington, D.C.: Law
Enforcement Assistance Administration, 1975).

justice planning process. It is clear that this effort has implications for federal, state, and regional planning authorities who will ultimately approve and fund the educational and research efforts that will be necessary to bring a higher level of planning sophistication to criminal justice agencies and their planners.

8

Gearing Up for Criminal Justice Planning

INTRODUCTION

The preceding chapters have almost exclusively dealt with the *content* problems of the embryonic profession of criminal justice planning. Little has been said about the organizational structure of planning, although organizational impediments to planning have been discussed. Let us conclude with a few remarks about the organization of the planning process in the criminal justice system.

Progress to Date

The summary report of the National Advisory Commission on Criminal Justice Standards and Goals contains a review of developments in justice planning that have grown out of the Safe Streets Act and LEAA.[1] That report describes the workings of the state criminal justice planning agencies (SPAs) that were mandated by federal legislation. In particular, the national commission stressed the failure of many state planning agencies to take a vigorous role in comprehensive planning. Those comments parallel some of the observations made at the beginning of this book, which noted that SPAs have often functioned more as conduits for federal funds than as planning agencies.

At the same time, the national commission did observe that some SPAs have played an important role as instruments for policy analysis and comprehensive reform. The commission then went on to argue for the broadening of the scope of planning at the state and local levels to include the entire budgetary picture and operations for all criminal agencies within specific jurisdictions, whether funded by LEAA or locally. Thus, one major recommendation was:

> The Commission recommends that SPA's develop by 1978 a general system of multiyear planning that takes into account all funds directed to crime control activities within the State.[2]

The national commission also emphasized the need for metropolitan and regional planning, offering a second recommendation:

> The Commission recommends that all major cities and counties establish criminal justice coordinating councils under the leadership of local chief executives.[3]

Finally, the national commission observed that criminal justice planning must reach beyond traditional police, courts, and corrections processes, to draw into the planning endeavor persons who are not justice system personnel. Specifically, the commission asserted:

> The Commission recommends that at least one-third of the membership of the State and local planning agency supervisory boards and

---

[1] National Advisory Commission on Criminal Justice Standards and Goals, *A National Strategy to Reduce Crime* (Washington, D.C., 1973).

[2] Ibid., p. 34.

[3] Ibid., p. 35.

councils be from officials of non-criminal justice agencies and from private citizens.

The Commission recommends that criminal justice planning agencies request direct written communications from operating agencies to assist them in defining the jurisdiction's objectives, needs, problems, and priorities. Temporary exchanges of personnel between criminal justice planning agencies and operating agencies should be undertaken on a regular basis.[4]

These recommendations of the national commission are eminently reasonable and accurately reflect the letter and spirit of the Safe Streets Act, which anticipated comprehensive planning based on broad input from representatives of the criminal justice field as well as nonprofessionals with an equal stake in crime prevention and control programs.[5]

The planning process so strongly encouraged by the national commission has not yet been fully realized. Writing as an LEAA staff member, Ewing has acknowledged that LEAA itself has undoubtedly contributed to the difficulties states have faced in undertaking comprehensive planning consistent with the recommendations of the national commission.[6] States have received mixed messages from LEAA that have resulted in planners' deciding to ignore system planning and concentrate on distribution of LEAA funds. Ewing makes the point that state planning agencies were given two functions, comprehensive planning and allocation of funds:

A kind of Gresham's Law set in some states, from the point of view of those who sought a broader definition of planning, and a broader role for the SPA. The review of grant applications, the development of plans to spend grant money, and the monitoring and auditing of grants consumed most of the time and staff resources of the state planning agencies, leaving little time for planning. Thus the

---

[4] Ibid, p. 36.

[5] These recommendations are closely paralleled by those of the National Council on Crime and Delinquency. See "Comprehensive Criminal Justice Planning: A Policy Statement," *Crime and Delinquency*, 20 (January 1974), 10–14.

[6] Blair G. Ewing, "Criminal Justice Planning: An Assessment," *Criminal Justice Review*, 1 (Spring 1976), 121–39.

narrower definition of planning was reinforced, and the planning function starved.[7]

As described earlier in this book, the compromise that appears to have taken place at operating state and regional planning levels can be characterized as a type of "ad hoc opportunism." Broad goals for the criminal justice system have been devised, but in actual fact, planners, policy boards, and agencies have to a large extent continued to confine their planning to specific program improvements according to a general set of priorities. In short, some criminal justice agencies continue to approach planning as a ready way to improve efficiency or to compensate for long-existing program deficiencies. More often than not, the result is "more of the same" for operating agencies, and innovative or strategic planning remains an ideal far removed from reality. Let us hope that Ewing's optimistic prediction of the emergence of an integrated, systemwide planning process will be realized. We agree with him that such a planning process is supported by congressional intent and LEAA guidelines, but the question remains whether this level of commitment is the substance or the shadow of what is occurring in the action crucible of state and local criminal justice planning and programs.

The Planner's Role

And what of the role of the planner in the turbulent arena of criminal justice planning? What perspective should the planner have in relation to the criminal justice system? Should the planner be passive, active, or reactive in response to the multiple pressures experienced from the many corners of the planning world? Should the planner accept the criminal justice system for what it has been, or should one's sights be set on what it might or should be?

All planning process models imply change—that is, impacting upon, affecting, eradicating, or ameliorating a problem condition. Indeed, whether planners appreciate the role or not, they find that they themselves are a part of the change process. This is sometimes a particularly nettlesome role in the criminal justice field, where value polarizations exist and where traditional functions and operational "turfs" of criminal justice agencies are strongly fixed in the

---

[7] Ibid., p. 127.

minds of agency representatives themselves, as well as among those who constitute the planning policy and advisory bodies at state and regional levels. As a result, many actors in the planning scene are likely to ask: "Why should we change?" or "How should we change?" These questions arise among representatives of the police, judicial, and correctional components of the criminal justice system. In fact, change in criminal justice agencies of all kinds is most frequently given a limited interpretation centered on relatively minor improvements in agency efficiency and is much less often acknowledged to involve alterations in roles or institutional arrangements.

Criminal justice planners have sometimes been lulled into accepting a narrow definition of change that supports it only to the extent that improvement in agency or program efficiency is the major goal. This tunnel vision is now under attack: theorists, social commentators, and some visionaries within the criminal justice field are emphasizing the need for major changes in the activities and functions of long-standing social institutions. They contend that traditional social responses and problem-solving stratagems directed at lawbreakers are simply too outmoded to be appropriate to the crime reduction demands of a "postindustrial" society.

The few thousand planners who man the criminal justice planning enterprise today are an amalgam of persons with varied criminal justice experiences, business backgrounds and orientation, and educational accomplishments, along with a sprinkling of education and experience in planning *per se*. For the most part, these individuals are learning planning while doing planning, supported at one time or another by in-service training programs developed around the themes of planning theory and practice. But their exposure to planning is usually on the "firing line," and they must depend on their wits, intuition, and knowledge from previous experience to cope with the pluralistic world of planning reality. Much of the planner's activity is based on a "seat-of-the-pants" assessment of "what will work" and "what the system will tolerate."

The above comments express a series of dilemmas that are equally puzzling to longtime experienced planners who have engaged in the planning process in other fields and who have concluded that planning as a profession is in constant transition.

What is different about planning in the criminal justice system is that it is new; it is emerging; it has an unrecognizable tradition. The criminal justice planner is a novice in a newly constructed planning arena where the participants are equally naive about the importance of planning in the present and even less certain about the potential of planning in the future. However, the planner cannot consider his or her plight unique, since the planning realities that must be confronted have been encountered in the past and in the present by others in other planning settings. All of this is to say that the criminal justice planner must not be overwhelmed by the array of apparently unresolvable dilemmas. Rather, as urged earlier in this book, the problems call for study of the considerable literature on planning theory and practice that has evolved over the recent past and is being added to at the present time. It follows that the criminal justice planner, drawing on experience in a specialized planning area, will ultimately be in a position to learn from existing knowledge and to make contributions to this growing knowledge base over time.

But if the dilemmas faced by the criminal justice planner are real and if they cannot be resolved magically, how then can they at least be "managed"? The answer to this question is that they are being and will be managed. The complex criminal justice system, while it is fragmented and most often functioning as a nonsystem, has been significantly impacted by the LEAA efforts of the past few years. The definition of planning, for example, has been given a new dimension beyond the budget cycle. More formal interagency communications and even planning efforts are occurring. A wide variety of citizen reaction and input is being heard through the planning mechanisms developed at state and local levels. And, finally, this entire process has a cohesive agent operating in the form of federal dollars, allocated more recently on better evidence of systemwide planning.

The criminal justice planner may idealize a rational planning world, but that world does not exist anywhere for the social planner in our pluralistic society. The reality is one in which the criminal justice planner learns to play many roles simultaneously: at one time the bureaucrat whose decisions will reflect administrative realities, while at another time an interpreter, an organizer, a clarifier, and an enabler. In certain circumstances the planner will be an advocate or a supporter of the advocacy of others. Opportunism, too, will become the planner's option, to be balanced at other times by a willingness to stand alone when whipsawed by converging pressures from political, community, and agency forces. From this perspective, the planner will manage dilemmas by playing an assortment of roles, not only in the formulation of the comprehensive plan but in its implementation as well. The technology that the planner will depend on is more rudimentary than cast in rules and formulas; it is a combination of hypotheses, theories, and tested case findings. Planning is, to put it simply, a quasi-profession in which tensions, conflicts, and dilemmas are the warp and woof of everyday existence. Planning is a coping profession.

GEARING UP FOR PLANNING

In spite of the time, energy, and money that has been spent since the inception of the Safe Streets Act in 1968, pessimism prevails concerning the national effort to establish viable crime and delinquency prevention, control, and treatment programs. The range of issues characterizing the criminal justice field today can be viewed as symptomatic of variations on the theme of planning inadequacy that is equally applicable to most institutions in our society as they face the impact of social forces over which they have little control. Michael has directed attention to this situation by noting that our societal condition is "historically unique" and urges a changeover from a fragmented and incremental problem-solving mentality to a focus on "future-responsive societal planning," by which he means a turning from conventional piecemeal problem solving to systems planning, with innovative goals replacing expedient goals.[8] He is joined in his argument by Friedmann, who emphasizes that in the decades ahead the traditional societal-guidance system will no longer suffice but must be replaced by a planning system that extends participatory roles far beyond what we are accustomed to and establishes as ends new approaches to societal guidance.[9]

As viewed by theorists such as Michael and Friedmann, this approach calls for a new perspective on planning in which the planning function itself is given a new "power" status in developing change strategies, involving at the same time much broader participation by the citizenry. Overlaying this approach on the criminal justice system will undoubtedly bring about new tensions and even confusion, judging from the first planning steps the criminal justice system components have taken under the Safe Streets Act. Neverthe-

---

[8] Donald N. Michael, On Learning to Plan—And Planning to Learn (San Francisco: Jossey-Bass, 1973).

[9] John Friedmann, Retracking America (Garden City, N.Y.: Anchor Books/ Doubleday, 1973).

less, the planning process cannot be learned in a sterile laboratory and subsequently applied to real-life situations. Those involved in the criminal justice system, just as those involved in other institutional systems, must "learn planning while doing planning," gaining at the same time a new understanding of the dimensions of planning and the process skills essential to plan development and implementation.

While it is difficult to chart a clear planning direction for the criminal justice field, it is possible to extrapolate from the thinking of planning theorists such as Bolan,[10] Michael, and Friedmann to suggest that the planning foundation that has been developed at state and local levels under LEAA be expanded and complemented to represent a "system planning network." Such a system will of necessity have to move beyond the superficial planning focus of the present arrangement to impact eventually on criminal justice agency organizational structure, policy decisions, and program operations. By its very makeup, the system will require participation of professional planners, criminal justice representatives, and citizens who reflect the broad spectrum of community attitudes and ideals.

Burt Nanus has sketched a design for organization of planning:

We may approach the question of organizing for planning by contemplating an "ideal" future-oriented criminal justice agency. First of all, in such an agency, the top management would be committed to long-range planning as the principal vehicle for instituting organizational change and preventing purely reactive management. This implies that there would be a continual effort to clarify and articulate the department's purposes and goals. Second, there would be a permanent staff charged with preparing forecasts and projections of likely futures, facilitating the planning of the various divisions and bureaus in the agencies, and bringing to bear the growing body of new planning techniques to address the long-range problems of the agency. Third, there would be a data base consisting of future-oriented internal and external information for use in decision making in the agency. Fourth, no important decisions would be made without consideration of their possible future effects and without coordinating with other interfacing agencies affected by the decision. Finally, there would be an emphasis upon an ongoing research effort to help understand the structure and dynamics

---

[10] Richard S. Bolan, "Emerging Views of Planning," *Journal of the American Institute of Planners,* 33 (July 1967), 233–45.

of the agency and the way in which it interacts with its environment.[11]

We have some additional comments along this line, to add to
those of Nanus. As first steps in developing a planning network, the
following suggestions are seen as having the potential to generate an
improved criminal justice planning system:

Each criminal justice subcomponent agency should establish a "planning office" with personnel attuned to planning, systems, and organizational theory and methodology.

Comment: The planning office within the criminal justice agency
            must have equal status with other departmental divisions. The
            planning office director should likewise have the same voice
            in policy deliberations as other divisional directors. Planning
            office personnel should be selected primarily for their ex-
            pertise in planning theory and process rather than for their
            previous program experience or knowledge.

Each criminal justice subcomponent should define planning in terms
of intersystems focus and avoid entangling the planning staff solely in
project planning designed for immediate payoff.

Comment: Where criminal justice agencies have been successful in
            developing planning capability, the tendency has been to
            utilize this expertise to plan projects. This has been particu-
            larly true when LEAA funding has been made available to
            underwrite agency program efforts. Such assignments have
            more often than not been concerned with project proposal
            writing aimed at addressing an agency program need or crisis.
            While project development may be a reasonable part of a.
            planning perspective, it should be encompassed within a
            planning operation that includes intersystem goals and ob-
            jectives.

Each criminal justice subcomponent should develop a planning advisory committee to include representatives of other criminal justice
agencies and citizens-at-large.

Comment: The relative isolation of individual criminal justice agen-
            cies makes it imperative to have intersystem and citizen input
            into the planning process. The agency planning advisory

---

[11] Burt Nanus, "A General Model for Criminal Justice Planning," *Journal
of Criminal Justice*, 2 (Winter 1974), 352.

committee, however, must be committed to more than formal
sanctioning of planning. The committee must engage itself
in "planned learning" of systems needs, system and agency
goals, and a planning process that identifies the strategic planning process as the reason for existence.

Planning advisory committees should be organized at both state and
local levels in conjunction with LEAA-funded planning mechanisms.

In addition to planning advisory committees attached to individual criminal justice agencies, committees selected from
members of agency planning committees should be developed
to work in support of state and local LEAA funded planning
staffs. The purpose of an interrelated planning structure at
state and local levels would be to provide the systems perspective needed in planning criminal justice programs. An
added advantage of a formal planning structure at these levels
would be the balance that can be given to the decision-making
process of stage and local policy making groups which can
be strongly influenced by individual agency and political
viewpoints.

A national planning advisory committee with a full-time staff should
be organized to function at the LEAA level.

It is not sufficient for the immediate and long range recommendations of the National Advisory Commission on Criminal Justice Standards and Goals to stand as the final word on
the direction of criminal justice planning. As experience
with LEAA funded planning accumulates and as a better
understanding of the criminal justice system in operation
evolves, it is crucial that a permanent planning mechanism
be established at the federal level to integrate state and local
planning knowledge into further directions for the criminal
justice system. The National Advisory Commission's standards
and goals are a first step in this direction but the effort needs
to be sustained as a key part of integrated national, state, and
local planning mechanisms.

SOME OBSERVATIONS ON POLICY BOARDS

With the passage of the Omnibus Crime Control legislation in 1968,
a new dimension of accountability was added to the criminal justice
field and its component agencies. The federal legislation made man-

datory the establishment of a state-level "policy" board in every state and territory. This concept was later expanded to the local and district levels where networks of policy boards have been developed, having the responsibility for participating in decisions on programs and fund distribution that affect most criminal justice agencies in the community.

The significance of this new network of policy-level bodies cannot be ignored in any consideration of criminal justice planning. The membership, structure, and activities of these groups have major consequences for the planning and programs of all criminal justice agencies, whether they are beneficiaries of LEAA funding or not. It is important, therefore, to examine the character of board structure and assess those boards in terms of criteria that have evolved from the experience of other boards in both the public and private sectors.

One organization outside of the field of criminal justice which has had long experience in observing and assessing the operations of voluntary boards is the Child Welfare League of America. As a national voluntary standard-setting agency in the child welfare field, the league has had a long history of involvement with direct service and volunteerism in the social services. Over the years it has paid particular attention to the structure and functions of social agency boards, and it has developed guidelines for board organization and activities that have direct implications for the guidance of the state and district boards that have developed under the federal crime control legislation.[12]

Speaking specifically of social agency boards, the league noted that prior to the 1960s, the traditional and legal role of a board of directors was one in which board members saw their tasks as centering on policymaking, fund raising, and giving advice to management:

> What agencies needed and sought were board members who could bring influence and affluence to insure that the agencies were adequately funded, who could interpret its services, and who could serve as advocates for child welfare services and for the agencies as they continued to seek sanction, legitimation, acceptance and rewards for their agencies.[13]

Thus, notes the league, board members tended to be a blue-ribbon group, not fully representative of the community-at-large, but

---

[12] Child Welfare League of America, *Guide for Board Organization in Social Agencies* (New York, 1975).

[13] Ibid., p. viii.

whose concerns about the needs of children and whose status in the community and access to resources enabled them to effectively assist the agencies in reaching their goals. There was usually a high degree of consensus in their decision making.

In the 1960s, however, with the advent of the poverty programs under the federal Office of Economic Opportunity and kindred developments, a sharp break occurred with the past, under the concept of "maximum feasible participation" of the recipients of social services. The league notes that this movement brought about "a heightened understanding of human beings as initiators in social processes, not passive particles in the grip of social situations . . ."[14] According to the league:

> In this new search for participation, problems of institutional governance were sharpened because of the breakdown of the previous consensus that followed the inclusion in these boards of other groups that challenged many of the traditional values and assumptions of social institutions, including child welfare organizations. The concept developed that boards of directors should be more broadly responsible. Employees, consumers, minority-group persons, women and young people all demanded that child welfare agencies (as well as other social institutions) pay more attention to their views and interests. In response to this demand for public accountability, some agencies added members of these groups to their boards of directors. The function of these new-type board members was twofold: (1) to broaden the perspective of the governing and/or advisory board since some members came from different backgrounds and experiences, and had intimate knowledge of the life style and problems of the group that was being served; (2) to enable the new directors to act as monitors for the public at large, as if they were the public's "window into the agency."[15]

The league analysis goes on to note that these expanded boards, which were supposed to bring about more participatory governance, were often plagued at the beginning with conflicts of interest and ideological quarrels, such that the board members pulled and tugged at each other, rather than engaging in cooperative man-

---

[14] Ibid., p. 1x.

[15] Ibid, pp. ix–x.

agement and guidance of agency affairs. But, in many cases, board directors eventually developed greater competence and breadth of knowledge and began to function with greater assertiveness and wisdom. Also, many of the new recruits to boards, selected from previously excluded groups, gradually learned a good deal about how to function as board members, rather than as advocates of narrow constituency interests. Some board members, however, found these new experiences, which called upon them to engage in meaningful dialogue with a more representative sampling of the citizenry, to be traumatic and ultimately dropped out of board activity.

The period since the 1960s has been one of adjustment and less conflict in the social service field. Clearly, the social movements of the 1960s have had an effect on board structure and functions in both the public and private sectors in that representation on such boards is now broader and more representative of community interests. It is interesting to note that the Omnibus Crime Control legislation did not mandate that ex-offenders be members of state- or local-level policy groups, although many such bodies do include former criminal justice system recipients on their boards. The functional emphasis of current boards is to a larger extent than in the past on management and fiscal accountability, goal-oriented planning, community-wide communication, and program evaluation. This is as true of private social service agencies as it is of criminal justice policy boards established under the aegis of LEAA.

Implications for Criminal Justice Policymaking

We can synthesize an assortment of information that can be applied to the policy bodies that now exist in the criminal justice field from the Child Welfare League and related management literature on the organization and functions of policy boards. We begin with the assumption that such groups have clear authority to exist and perform stated functions usually mandated and described in state and/or local legislation or executive orders. More specific elaboration of the functions is usually then spelled out in bylaws reviewed and adopted by the individual boards.

The policy boards established under the Omnibus Crime Control legislation on the state and local levels would ordinarily have the following responsibilities:

1. Selection of board members (through a nominating committee process) who are representative of the criminal justice field and the community-at-large.

2. Selection of the planning agency director (or approval if the director is selected by the political governing body), and subsequent assessment of the performance of the agency director on the basis of a written work performance description.

3. Governance of the planning agency through development of broad policies and planning objectives. (Planning objectives in state and local criminal justice agencies are currently modeled after the standards and goals in the 1973 publication of the National Advisory Commission on Criminal Justice Standards and Goals.) Implicit in this policymaking function is the advocacy role that the criminal justice planning board may have to take at a given point in time with criminal justice agencies, political decision makers, and the broader community.

4. Review and approval of accountability mechanisms that will allow the board to have knowledge of the degree to which planning objectives are being achieved and fiscal management responsibilities met.

As noted in other sections of this book, these responsibilities call for board members who have expertise in their particular field, who have broad knowledge of and interest in the entire criminal justice system, or who exhibit a degree of objectivity that will permit them to avoid parochialism in the decision-making process. Although some degree of dissent is inevitable, board members must be able to conduct their board roles within a system and community perspective that extends beyond narrow self-interests. The history of criminal justice planning, unhappily, is replete with examples of the latter focus where policy planning board members at state and local levels have too often become extensions of specific agencies and have become absorbed in the details of proposal reviews and dollar juggling, very often to assure funding to agencies they represent or to reflect a particular program bias. Criminal justice planning boards must move away from this pattern toward a broader definition of functions.

CONCLUDING COMMENTS

The most serious limitation of the series of recommendations in this chapter and elsewhere in this book is that even with implementation, the planning system itself may not reach beyond the limited spectrum of criminal justice agency operations. As noted earlier, these operations have been based strongly on the intervention recipes and strategies of the 1950s and 1960s, rather than moving in the direction of truly innovative and imaginative criminal justice programs. What is implicit in these recommendations, however, is that the expanded planning mechanism must be cross-fertilized with the knowledge of theorists from the fields of economics, social science, and planning itself. The objective of the total planning mechanism would be to develop "visionary planners" in the persons of professionals and non-professionals engaged in the planning process who can begin to grapple with the larger social trends in American society and their implications for criminal justice. At the professional level particularly, the planning task ahead calls for individuals who can wed planning theory and practice rather than function simply as criminal justice mechanics. Comprehensive and innovative planning will be stalled at the inception level if the system itself does not eventually provide the forum for exchange and weighing of knowledge and applying it to influence the criminal justice field and beyond.

The final thrust of these comments is that increased attention needs to be given to the development and dissemination of a viable knowledge base for justice planning practice within the criminal justice doctoral programs in the United States where professional planners are being trained. Innovative and comprehensive planning cries out for the creation of a vital partnership between those from the world of ideas and those from the world of practical matters. It will only be through efforts of this kind that it may someday be possible to transform justice planning from a relatively crude art form into a profession with the capacity to have a significant impact on the crime and delinquency problem in modern society.

Index